Landscaping
Your Vacation Place

Jack Kramer

Charles Scribner's Sons   New York

Copyright © 1975 Jack Kramer

LIBRARY OF CONGRESS CATALOGING IN PUBLICATION DATA

Kramer, Jack, 1927-
 Landscaping your vacation place.

 1. Landscape gardening.   2. Summer homes.
I. Title.
SB473.K74   712'.6   74-11228
ISBN 0-684-13959-6
ISBN 0-684

1 3 5 7 9 11 13 15 17 19 MD/C 20 18 16 14 12 10 8 6 4 2
1 3 5 7 9 11 13 15 17 19 M/P 20 18 16 14 12 10 8 6 4 2

Printed in the United States of America

Contents

Introduction:
Your Home Away From Home

The idea for this book began many years ago when a friend loaned me his summer house in Traverse City, Michigan. He said the house was free to me for a few weeks if I'd do a little work in the neglected garden, and indeed some gardening was necessary when I saw the house and site. My friend had started his garden all wrong. Many of the plants were inappropriate for the climate; the plan itself was complicated and required too much time to maintain, especially for the vacationer. There was little I could do and yet the house inside was so lively that appropriate green touches were needed outdoors. I made notes and sketches so the following year my friend could start gardening with an eye on beauty and ease of maintenance. And this is what this book is all about—knowing your site, starting with the right plants that will grow for you rather than you working for them, and then keeping the garden with little effort.

When you select a vacation place, it is generally in unfamiliar surroundings; climate and rainfall, temperature and soil, are different from what you have normally worked with. So it is wise to know a little about your place before you dig in. Furthermore, I think everyone likes his vacation retreat to be as attractive as possible. Whether it is a cabin in the forest, a small desert place, a house in the country, or a seaside structure, different conditions will face the vacation gardener. Even mobile homes and condominiums need some planting to make them a home away from home.

In LANDSCAPING YOUR VACATION PLACE I tell you just what plants will grow where, whether you are at the seaside, in the forest, in the desert or in a temperate all year climate. For each locale there are specific plans and plantings to make your vacation home appealing and to save you needless garden work. I include extensive lists of plants for each location and also lists of special time-saving plants, such as ground covers, vines, and bulbs and plants for container gardening—over 550 plants in all. So whether you want to garden on weekends only, or just a day a week (and relax the rest of the time) you will find your guide to better vacation gardening in this book.

JACK KRAMER

LANDSCAPING YOUR VACATION PLACE

BY THE SEA, IN THE DESERT, IN TEMPERATE CLIMATES, IN FOREST, OR ON HILLSIDE

1. Vacation Homes

A vacation house is a retreat from your usual surroundings, a place to get away to on weekends or a place to spend a few weeks (as many as possible) during the year. Or a vacation home may be a second home where you spend 3 or 6 months of the year. In any case, each place requires different gardening procedures.

Years ago people rented vacation houses—a house by the sea, a place in the country—but today more and more of these houses are being purchased. And these homes away from home used to be primitive, with a minimum of convenience, but now they are much more sophisticated. However, no matter what a vacation represents to you, you will want one that is attractive and conducive to relaxation, which means plants and landscaping.

The gardening aspect of vacation homes appeals to many people, but when gardening in different regions the vacationer finds himself facing an entirely new kind of gardening in a new soil under unfamiliar conditions. Thus, *where* the vacation house is will dictate just what kind of gardening you can do; this, of course, varies from region to region. For simplicity we have classified regions as (1) by the sea, (2) in the desert, (3) in the hills and forests, and (4) in year-round, temperate climates. But even within these classifications there are variants in growing plants in, say, a 100-mile radius.

Where It Is

The vacation house is usually selected according to geographical preference. Some people like to be, or must be, within a short distance of their everyday home. Others usually choose a climate opposite to

1

This elegant seaside garden of roses and perennials is beautifully landscaped and yet it is small enough for minimum maintenance. Note the walls to help thwart strong winds and the path that defines the garden; altogether a handsome picture by the sea. (*Photo by Roche*).

the one they live in; for example, the Easterner or Midwesterner might migrate to California, Florida, or the desert. It is important to realize that each region—in the country, by the sea, in the desert—will present a different kind of gardening. Do not think that the plants you grew in Chicago will thrive in Arizona, or the garden you had in southern Georgia will survive on the Pacific Coast. It cannot be done. Your chosen location will dictate just what you can and cannot grow.

Quite logically, many people are drawn to the seaside; ironically, this is the most difficult site for plants. Seaside gardening has many hazards, including wind and rain, sudden storms and erosion, all factors that can make gardening a nightmare. But gardening by the sea can be enjoyable. There are many plants that can and indeed do thrive in such conditions, but you must know what plants to use and how to treat them. After all, you do not want to spend all your vacation time gardening; play and relaxation are important considerations.

The desert garden can also be a harsh environment for plants, cool at night but blazing hot during the day. Wind storms can play havoc with plants, and droughts may be frequent. Sudden rains are another hazard, so more than any other place, the desert vacation home—generally devoid of plant life, needs some greenery to make it a place to relax and enjoy. Again, your choice of plants will determine whether you succeed or fail.

Hillsides or mountains (and many people are especially fond of these areas for vacationing) represent yet another way and kind of gardening. Gardening on hills and slopes requires careful landscape planning unless you are a mountain goat. Yet in these regions there are many easy-to-grow plants that can quickly make an Eden out of the site.

Gardening in year-round temperate areas presents still another *modus operandi* because in warm climates plants flourish. Yet they

A beautiful example of matching house to the site is shown in this contemporary vacation house in a wooded hillside setting. The landscaping has been left natural; only some native shrubs were added at left of deck, and a small garden area taking advantage of level land in rear is for the garden. (*Photo courtesy California Redwood Assoc.*).

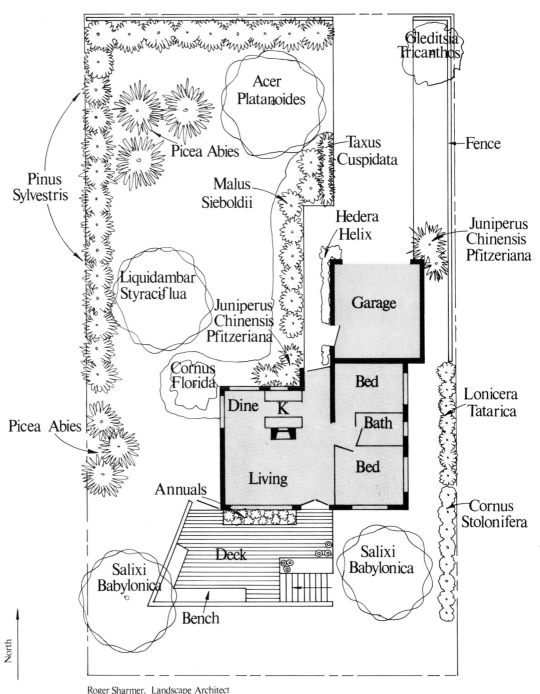

Acer
Platanoides

Picea Abies

Pinus
Sylvestris

Liquidambar
Styraciflua

Juniperus
Chinensis
Pfitzeriana

Picea Abies

Cornus
Florida

Taxus
Cuspidata

Malus
Sieboldii

Hedera
Helix

Gleditsia
Tricanthos

Fence

Juniperus
Chinensis
Pfitzeriana

Garage

Bed

Dine   K

Bath

Bed

Living

Lonicera
Tatarica

Cornus
Stolonifera

Annuals

Deck

Salixi
Babylonica

Salixi
Babylonica

Bench

North

Roger Sharmer, Landscape Architect
Rendering by Jim Carew

Cottage

still require planting and trimming and, above all, an intelligent selection of plant life.

Gardening in the forest is perhaps the easiest landscape to manage because, if you do not feel like gardening, you can let nature take its course. Some trimming and pruning will be necessary occasionally, but basically native plants make for an easy-to-care-for garden.

No matter what area your vacation home is in (unless it is a totally new site), there will probably be trees and shrubs—plant life in some form. It is a good idea to take stock of just what is there and to try and save as much as possible. Trees definitely should not be removed unless absolutely necessary, and shrubs should be saved, pruned, and rejuvenated in lieu of major removal. Save what you have because you will be surprised at what you can coax back to health with tender loving care.

WHAT KINDS OF HOUSES
There are variations in types of vacation houses: shell houses; pre-fabricated houses, where everything is furnished except plumbing and electricity; manufactured houses, which include a variety of types and custom homes. Each house has a different character, and each house will dictate what kind of landscape plan to follow. The furnishings inside the house must be in harmony with the structure, and the outdoor furnishings (plants and trees) must also blend with the type of house. For example, a small cottage by the sea needs a different kind of landscape plan than the house in the country, and a small A-frame house in the mountains requires yet another setting. Some vacation homes are contemporary, and thus a garden somewhat formal in character will be the ideal marriage. A Swiss chalet-type vacation home landscape will borrow a little from the formal, a lot from the natural landscape plan. So before you start any planting, determine just what kind of house you have, what the shape of the property is, and then decide on the proper landscape plan to complement the setting. A few trees and shrubs here and there do not make a landscape plan. You must strive for easy gardening rather than gardening on a full scale.

Gardens have a particular feeling or style. Those with flower borders and small trees tend to be charming and intimate, suitable to the cottage. Other garden plans may be composed of evergreens, larger

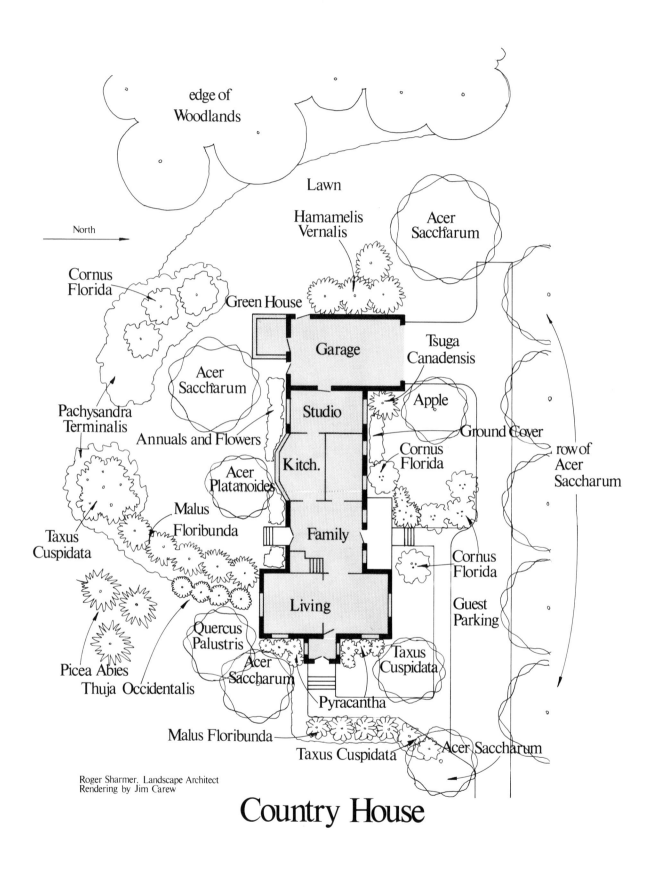

edge of
Woodlands

Lawn

North

Hamamelis
Vernalis

Acer
Saccharum

Cornus
Florida

Green House

Garage

Tsuga
Canadensis

Acer
Saccharum

Apple

Pachysandra
Terminalis

Studio

Ground Cover

Annuals and Flowers

Kitch.

Cornus
Florida

Acer
Platanoides

Malus
Floribunda

Family

Taxus
Cuspidata

Cornus
Florida

Living

Guest
Parking

Quercus
Palustris

Acer
Saccharum

Taxus
Cuspidata

Picea Abies
Thuja Occidentalis

Pyracantha

Malus Floribunda

Taxus Cuspidata

Acer Saccharum

row of
Acer
Saccharum

Roger Sharmer. Landscape Architect
Rendering by Jim Carew

Country House

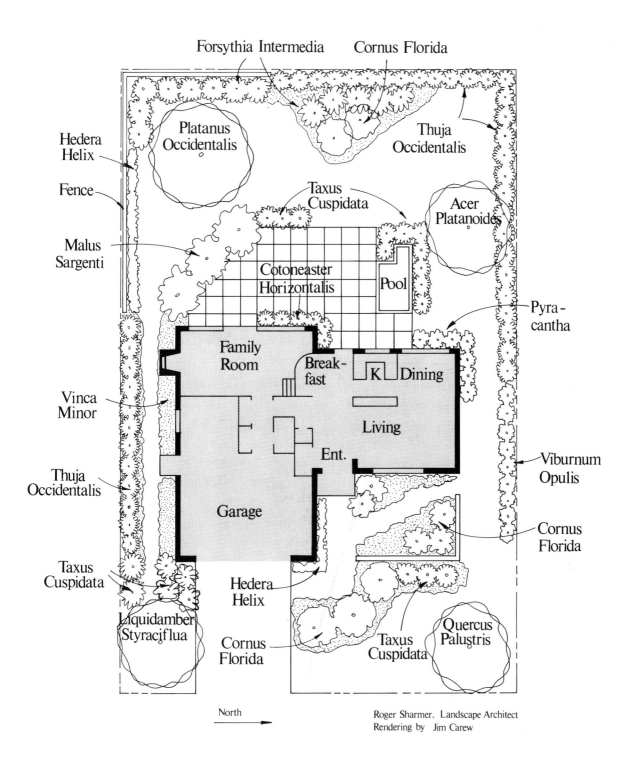

Forsythia Intermedia

Cornus Florida

Hedera Helix

Platanus Occidentalis

Fence

Thuja Occidentalis

Malus Sargenti

Taxus Cuspidata

Acer Platanoides

Cotoneaster Horizontalis

Pool

Pyra-cantha

Vinca Minor

Family Room

Break-fast

K Dining

Living

Ent.

Viburnum Opulis

Thuja Occidentalis

Garage

Cornus Florida

Taxus Cuspidata

Hedera Helix

Liquidamber Styraciflua

Cornus Florida

Taxus Cuspidata

Quercus Palustris

North

Roger Sharmer, Landscape Architect
Rendering by Jim Carew

Small House

This house, in temperate all-year climate, is sparsely but finely landscaped for easy maintenance. Trees frame the structure on each side complemented by smaller trees in the rear. Shrubs in front of the house with rock walls balance a totally fine landscape plan. (*Photo courtesy American Plywood Association*).

Low and blending into the landscape, a contemporary vacation house uses the natural backdrop of nature as landscaping. A few small trees have been added at left to balance the setting. (*Photo by Phokian Karas; Architect: Andrew Daland, AIA*).

trees and shrubs, and fewer flowers; this plan would be suitable for, say, a country house at the edge of the woods. The native garden, where stress is put in natural plant materials, is more in keeping with a small rustic house in the forest. Again, each landscape plan has a definite feeling, and each house has a certain character. The meshing of the two is what will produce an attractive house and garden.

In addition to the house and its landscape plan, the site—the shape of the property—will play a large part in the final plan. For example:

Long, narrow lot. At first glance this may seem like a limited area

Shrubs and trees cradle this handsome vacation home in the forest. Native plants are emphasized and maintenance of plantings is minimal. (*Photo courtesy Boise Cascade Co., Kingsbury Homes*).

for a successful plan. But it has advantages because it can be easily sectioned into individual areas. Each part of the plan can be pulled together to form a harmonious landscape. Geometrical shapes work well for this type of lot, and a charming plan can be created. Avoid very large trees and shrubs and masses of flowers.

Rectangular lot. This common type of lot is one of the easiest to work with. Generally, intelligent screening (fences and hedges) is necessary to achieve a private setting. Because the space is somewhat confining and monotonous, plan areas with paving and stepping stones to provide line and form. Use bushy plants to give mass and grace to the area.

Wedge-shaped lot. A desirable situation is the narrow end toward the street because it leaves most of the property behind the house, where all kinds of garden structures can be set up. This site allows a large varied garden plan of many interests.

Corner lot. This is considered a choice site, yet it presents a difficult landscaping challenge. Both the side and the front are open to the public, and private space is lost. Court entries and interesting galleries can be used to compensate for lost space.

2. *Preparing the Property*

A garden depends upon the soil—every plant will live, grow, or die in it. If you have a new vacation home, before any planting can be started, rough grading and leveling must be done so there is proper run-off of excess water. This is the time to plan and decide what you want, to observe and determine just what has to be done to ensure trouble-free landscaping. Many new homes have a naked feeling, and the owner is faced with a vacation cabin or house that is not ready for landscaping and is hardly a beautiful setting—just yet.

GRADING AND LEVELING

Grading controls erosion, thus ensuring proper water drainage. Grading is also necessary to make level areas for outdoor living and to provide planting areas that will not cause trouble later. This may all seem like a costly procedure, but it is absolutely necessary to start out correctly so you do not spend all your vacation time gardening.

Many times, when the contractor leaves the site, the subsoil is several inches below the house; this subsoil must be filled in so that the slope of the land will carry off excess water. Also, the topsoil may have been removed or pushed aside in a gigantic hill during the construction of the house. If you had a considerate contractor, the moved topsoil may still be on the site. If it is gone, you will have to replenish it, an expensive undertaking: an average site of a half acre can require as much as 80 yards of topsoil.

However, before you do anything about topsoil, the lot must be graded and leveled. A large area will require the help of a rented bulldozer or front-end loader. Not much grading will be needed on a

This new garden shows grading and level operation; some shrubs are in place and evergreens are against the far fence. The level expanse will be used as a lawn to provide a green carpet for the house. (*Photo by author*).

level lot before you start unless there is to be a pool or a terrace. But more grading is needed on a sloping or hillside lot if you intend to use that part of the property (and it is nice to have paths and walks through the grounds). On a small lot you can do some grading yourself with a rake and shovel. Break up stones, remove all trash, and smooth and level all mounds and hollows.

Rough grading refers to the moving and shaping of the contour of the lot. If the existing level is high, it must be sheared off; if it is low, it must be filled in. Once the fence is up and the shrubbery in place at the boundaries, it is impossible to get equipment in to grade the areas. Determine at the start where you want the terrace; decide now where a flat surface for flower beds is needed (and I do suggest you have a cutting garden because cut flowers make a vacation cheerful).

Leveling is done when the grading is finished. It is the process of smoothing and leveling the ground so there are no hollows or hills.

If you have an old house, grading, leveling, and drainage have withstood the test of time. You can assume that there will be no more investment aside from secondary projects. Perhaps you will have to bring in some topsoil or make a few changes, but the cost will be nothing like the investment involved in preparing the new lot for planting.

Drainage

Rainwater must be able to drain off your property because hollows create bogs, and rises are unsightly. A flooded vacation home is hardly something to look forward to on weekends! The ground should slope away from the house to carry water to the nearest street, storm drain, or watercourse. The finished surface should be flat, without rises or hollows. Be sure the slope is in one direction, toward

The level area of this house has been graded for a patio. Here wood forms are put in place with concrete to be poured later. The patio area was planned with the house, making it an easy installation. (*Photo by author*).

Vinca is used as a soil binder for this house on a hill. The ground cover is maintenance free after installation and provides a sea of green. (*USDA Photo*).

either the street or rear. Where the water runoff is more than the ground can handle without causing erosion, ditches can be dug at the edge of the property in inconspicuous places to collect the water and channel it to a lower area, where it can seep away.

Until you have had some rain or a spring thaw, it is difficult to determine just how much work has to be done to provide adequate drainage. In a new site that has been excavated and filled in, the natural drainage patterns have been interrupted. You do not know where the water will go and where it will run off your property (perhaps to cause problems on a neighbor's land). Try to determine the natural slope of the land where water would run off, and grade the land accordingly.

SOIL

Soil is the basis of gardening. Light, air, and water are needed too, but these elements are for the taking. Only when the soil is properly prepared, that is of a balanced nutritional mix, can you start to landscape.

There are three kinds of soil: clay, which is heavy; sandy, which is light; and loam, which is porous. Just what kind of soil you have depends upon where your vacation home is located geographically.

Sandy soil is easy to work with and warms up quickly in spring, but it will not hold moisture because water goes through it so fast plants cannot absorb it. Adding liberal quantities of organic matter will improve a sandy soil.

A very sandy subsoil that retains little moisture is useless to plants. If it is very claylike, it holds water so long that plants literally drown in it. It should be broken up, or in severe cases a drainage system may have to be installed to carry off water.

Top soil is composed of small particles of disintegrated rock, minerals, and decomposing organic matter. Most soils lose their mineral content over the years, and unless you are on fertile land the soil must be reworked and revitalized.

A fertile soil that is a mixture of clay, sand, and humus is porous in texture and provides good drainage; this is the kind of soil plants will thrive in. It is spongy, so it retains moisture, and it has humus, so it provides good conditions for the growth of soil bacteria (nutri-

These soil samples show three kinds of soil: clay on left, sandy soil in center and porous crumbly soil on right. (*USDA Photo*).

ents) for plants. But in most cases this kind of soil must be built up by a program of soil conditioning.

Soil Conditioning. Humus—animal manure, compost, leaf mold, peat moss—is decayed organic matter. It is an essential ingredient of a good soil. Humus adds body to sandy soils and provides aeration for clay soils. Humus is constantly used and depleted and so must be replaced to maintain healthy plant growth. Peat moss is available at nurseries. A second source of humus is leaf mold (decayed leaves and grass clippings). You can rake leaves into a pile and let them decompose, to use in your garden. You can also collect leaf mold from forests or buy it in tidy sacks—expensive though it is, it saves time.

Another excellent source of humus is compost, which is decayed vegetable matter of many kinds. Adding compost to soil is an easy way to keep improving it without much trouble. If you have time to make compost, select an inconspicuous place near the garden. Put up boards about 4 feet high to contain the compost, and leave an opening for a gate.

To start a humus pile, throw a few inches of manure into the bin, and then as you garden add grass clippings, dead flowers, leaves, and twigs. You can also add vegetable matter, eggshells, and other similar kitchen garbage. Keep the compost material in a mound, and add some more manure and a dusting of lime in a few weeks. Keep the materials sprinkled with water occasionally. Every so often turn the heap, bringing the sides to the top.

You must judge how much humus to add to soil because soils differ throughout the country. It will depend upon the soil and the kind of plants being grown. Generally, mix about 1 inch of humus to about 6 inches of soil.

In addition to the humus you add to the soil, also add fertilizers. Fertilizers contain nitrogen, phosphorus, and potassium (potash). But fertilizers are not substitutes for humus, nor can decayed organic matter completely do the work of fertilizers. Soil will need both.

When you visit your vacation site, dig up some soil and crumble it in your hand. If it is lumpy and claylike, you will need to add the necessary sand and humus. If it is sandy and falls apart in your hand, you will need to add some organic matter. A good soil crumbles in your hand and feels like a well-done baked potato: porous with good texture.

pH

The pH scale measures the acidity or alkalinity of soil. A pH of 7 is neutral; below 7 the soil is acid, and above 7 it is alkaline. Some commonly grown trees and shrubs grow in an alkaline soil or in acid conditions, but the majority of plants prefer a neutral soil. Thus, a soil reaction as nearly neutral as possible (between 6 and 7) will allow you to grow the most plants successfully.

Soil can be tested with an inexpensive soil test kit or if you send some soil to your local country agricultural agent he will analyze it for you. This may seem like a bother to the average person who is more interested in relaxing than gardening, but it can save a lot of

This soil is hard and claylike; it needs humus to make it friable and rich for plant life. (*USDA Photo*).

trouble when you do start landscaping the site (even on a small scale).

To lower the pH of soil (increase the acidity) use ground sulfur (at suppliers) at the rate of 1 pound to 100 square feet. This will lower the pH symbol of loam soil about 1 point. Spread the sulfur on top of the soil and then sprinkle with water. To raise the pH of soil (sweeten it) add ground limestone at the rate of 10 pounds per 150 square feet. Scatter the limestone on the soil, or mix it well with the top few inches of soil, and water. It is best to add ground limestone or hydrated lime in several applications at 6- or 8-week intervals instead of using too much at one time.

3. Design, Planting, and Climate

Where do you start? What do you do to make your vacation retreat attractive? Too many people give hardly any thought to the outside of the house. They are more concerned about the house itself because it is the major cost. Yet no one wants a vacation house on a barren piece of ground; it simply is not esthetically pleasing and does not impart a relaxed feeling. Green plants are necessary, so some design and planting must be considered, even on a minimum basis.

By all means let the house be the prime consideration, but keep a peripheral outlook on the terrain and the kind of landscape that will be possible when you are buying or renting your retreat. There are certain things you can determine by walking the property a few times that will help you in gardening.

The main consideration will be just what is already there, pre-supposing you are purchasing an existing house. (New houses require different considerations as outlined in Chapter 2.) It is easy to draw a rough sketch of existing plant material, shape of lot, and where the house sits. Simply put round circles in for trees, smaller circles for shrubs, and any other forms to designate flower beds and so on. And always keep in mind prevailing wind direction and sun orientation because they are prime factors in choosing and selecting plants.

DESIGN AND LANDSCAPING

The word landscaping frightens people; it sounds professional and denotes money. Do not let this thwart your gardening plans. You can get inexpensive professional advice from landscape architects in one or two consultations. Many times local nurseries have a service, and neighbors too can tell you what will or will not grow in the area. Even if you can not get professional help, you yourself can plan the property (and rightly you should because it is your home). Following are some basic landscape and design principles that should make things easier for you.

For the sake of simplicity divide the lot into individual areas for easy planning; do one at a time. Usually a first consideration will be the approach to the house. This is where the tempo is set for the rest of the house, so this area should be charming and inviting. Secondly, consider an outdoor living area, which can be a small patio or terrace or just a clearing where you can sit and relax. Thirdly, allow a functional service area where there will be places for cars, driveways, and easy access to the house for hauling groceries.

Now observe where the property boundaries are (always ask for a plot plan when purchasing). You will want to use as much of the property as possible. Visualize where walls and fences will be, or if

Small flowering trees and evergreens were planned for this unique vacation retreat. The heavily wooded plan softens the lines of the structure and the house is dramatic. Maintenance is minimal. (*Photo by Hedrich Blessing*); *Architect: Rodney Wright, AIA*).

they are necessary at all. Take advantage of what natural conditions are offered, such as a rolling hill, a backdrop of stately trees, or, on the other hand, a close-by house that might require screening. Once again, note existing trees and shrubs; you will want to use as much plant material as possible. Renovating an entire garden takes years (and time), and you will not want to spend all your vacation time gardening.

What you want is to establish a minimum-maintenance gardening plan that will allow you to garden at your leisure, especially if you are at your vacation place only a few months a year. This may mean lots of evergreens, groundcovers, and plants that care for themselves rather than a great many annuals or flower borders.

As previously mentioned, develop the landscape plan in a style to harmonize with the architecture of the house. Remember that there is the formal look, the informal look, or the natural garden—perhaps take a little from each, depending upon the house itself.

PLANNING ON PAPER

No matter what kind of vacation house you choose, first plan the landscape on paper. This is basically putting mass, form, line, and volume to work. You are deciding between asymmetrical and symmetrical balance, and a pencil plan can tell you a lot in a little time. Plans drawn to scale are unnecessary; you can make a sketch. Using the plot plan as a guide, transpose the location of the house and the boundary onto graph paper. Let each square represent a foot. Draw the outline of the house, any steps, walks, and driveways, and *show existing trees and shrubs*.

Lay a sheet of tracing paper over the graph paper. Draw rough sizes and shapes of objects you want in your garden to make vacation life easy. This can include patios, barbecue areas, new trees and shrubs, planting beds, and maybe a vegetable garden. The irregular shapes you have drawn should start to relate to each other. If you are not pleased with the first arrangement, start over on a new sheet of tracing paper.

Here are some hints to help you use shape and form. These simple basic forms are responsible for all linear patterns that develop in the garden. From these any number of combination of patterns can be drawn.

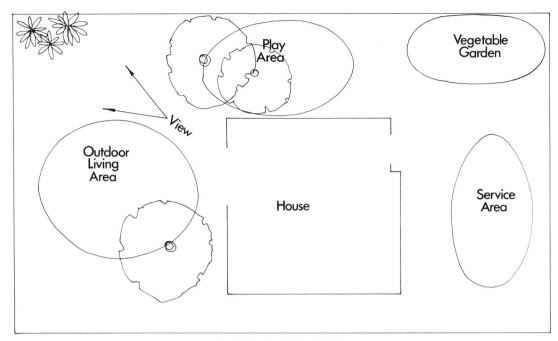

PRELIMINARY SKETCH

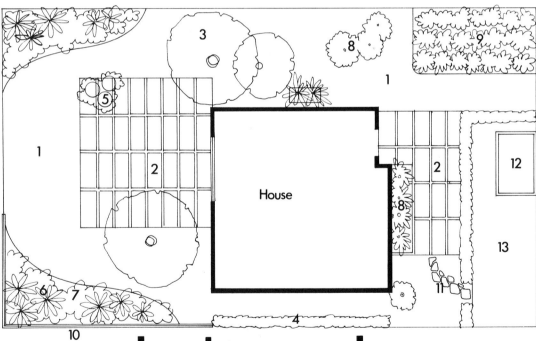

landscape plan

1 Lawn	5 Potted Plants	9 Vegetable Garden	13 Driveway
2 Patio	6 Misc. Plants	10 Fence	14 Steps
3 Tree	7 Ground Cover	11 Stone Paving	15 Wood Decking
4 Hedge	8 Shrub	12 Compost Bin	16 Fire Pit

1. Rectangular or square patterns are simple and most natural to use. They are usually projections of the house form. Work with a uniform module, that is, a space repeated again and again, to simplify a plan. The module can be 2 x 3 or 4 x 4 feet. The patio can be paved with 2 x 3 blocks, steppingstones can be the same size, and planting islands and beds can also relate to the same module. This is an easy way to establish proportion and harmony in quick fashion. There will be simplicity as well as concise organization.

2. Acute or obtuse angles or triangles reflect the angular form of the house and site, lead the eye to a focal point, and give a sense of space and direction.

3. Circular forms add interest to the pattern, and in proper balance with straight lines they can be pleasing compositions.

4. Free curves are curving, sweeping, natural lines of nature with constantly changing radius. They produce richness in motion.

PLANT MATERIALS

The plants you want for your vacation home are those that are easy to grow, so this means selecting plants that are appropriate for the conditions you can give them. Many plants will tolerate salt, wind, and a sandy soil, but many others simply will not or will require constant attention to survive. Plants for the desert garden must be carefully selected because many plants will not survive in these alkaline soils. In the forest or hillside locations, where there is much moisture and shade, you must select shade-loving, moisture-seeking specimens. By choosing the right plants, care will be at a minimum.

Native plants can certainly be used along with garden hybrids for all kinds of gardens. The natives are tough plants that have learned to survive through the centuries, and once established they will take care of themselves rather than you having to give them constant care.

If the situation is such that you decide to leave the surrounding landscape completely natural and do little gardening, consider growing container plants here and there for accents out in the grounds, or as decorative features on porches and decks. Container gardening has a great advantage over gardening in the ground because you can dictate the soil and move these portable gardens if light is too strong or too weak. (See Chapter 7.)

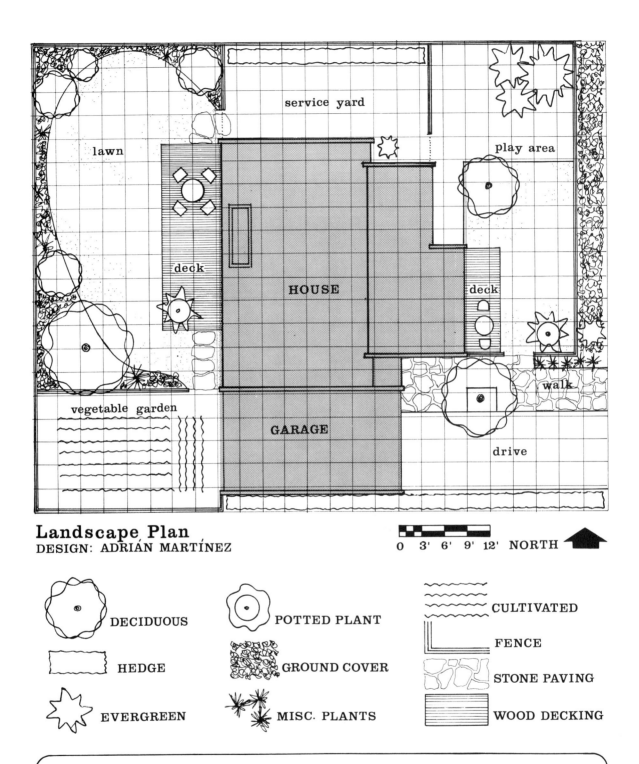

Landscape Plan
DESIGN: ADRIÁN MARTÍNEZ

0 3' 6' 9' 12' NORTH

DECIDUOUS

HEDGE

EVERGREEN

POTTED PLANT

GROUND COVER

MISC. PLANTS

CULTIVATED

FENCE

STONE PAVING

WOOD DECKING

Landscape Symbols

For the most part, try and buy your plant material from local nurseries. They will stock what grows best in the area and be able to help you select appropriate plants for your region. If such establishments do not exist in your area, you can buy plants from the many mail-order sources throughout the country, although even in this case it is best to purchase from nearby rather than distant sources.

Neighbors vacation gardens will tell you a great deal about just what will and will not grow in the region, so if possible arrange some visits to nearby homes. Make lists of plant materials and keep a record of notes. (See Chapter 5 for specific plants for specific areas.)

CLIMATE AND PLANTS

Climates vary greatly throughout the world. If you glance at a United States map of annual rainfall, you will see that there are very wet

A row of hydrangeas is the façade for this cabin; otherwise the land has been left natural and with little alteration. (*Photo by Matthew Barr*).

regions, moderately wet ones, arid locales, and so on. You must also consider how the rain falls. Is it heavy all year? Moderate, but heavy at times? Moderate in winter? Or is the rain scanty all year? Rain can be evenly distributed throughout the year, come in seasons, or it can come in the form of snow. Temperature varies from extreme heat in California's Death Valley to extreme cold in the Plains states. The USDA rain charts can tell you a great deal about your new site and can be obtained by writing the USDA, Washington, D.C. 20250. (There is a small fee.)

Today, many people have lost sight of what gardening really is. Too often the homeowner sprinkles granules, applies sprays, and feeds and protects his plants in a marathon program. None of the new products are miracle workers. Gardening still involves working with nature, and this means climate is the deciding factor of what will or will not grow for you. Turn back the pages. Take a lesson from your grandparents and be aware of the weather—be your own forecaster. Rainfall, sun, humidity, wind, and seasonal characteristics are all part of the gardening program. In every region climatic factors will differ. Even in a 10-mile radius climate can vary considerably, especially if you are near hills, lakes, and streams. For example, my house is only 14 miles from San Francisco. In summer it is 15 degrees warmer here than it is in the city. Our annual rainfall is about 38 inches, but in the city it is about 17 inches.

Similar climatic differences exist on the East Coast within its own regions. Some parts are quite hilly, and there are many lakes and streams that influence temperature, so take stock of the topography of your individual area. Rainfall will also vary considerably, as will the growing season. In the South, moderate all-year temperatures dictate another kind of gardening picture.

Be somewhat of a weatherman and pay attention to local weather forecasts, variable though they may be. This is not a book on climatology, but we are concerned with the general aspects of climate and its effect on plants; you will still have to temper the suggestions herein with knowledge of your climate. But this is not difficult to do. Any person who has lived in an area for a while can know something about rain and wind, temperature and humidity. If you are new in the area, ask a neighbor or the local nursery. And, of course,

Using native plants of the desert a patio area is the garden for the house; the area is small and beautifully landscaped for easy gardening. (*Photo by Gary Brant*).

the United States weather maps of your area will help you considerably.

Of course, climate can be modified somewhat. You cannot stop the wind, but you can stop its harmful effects. Prune trees properly to stop branch-breaking. Grow fruit trees espaliered against walls and fences, and put hedges in place to break the force of the wind.

If you are in a rainy area, drainage of excess water is very important, so proper facilities must be provided for. Soil is constantly leached, so be prepared to add fertilizer more often. In dry regions with scanty rainfall, soil must be improved, and you will have to pay more attention to watering plants.

If there is too much sun, plant under trees or to the north of the building (expect a reduction of flowering in plants). Try to provide a way to combat this great loss of moisture, which is the chief effect of excess sun. Mulching and protecting plants help a great deal. Although there are many superlative plants that will grow in your garden, you may not see them in other parts of your state. For example, the same plant against your house wall, protected from wind, may not grow on a hill above your house.

It is just good common sense to know how much wind to expect, and how and where the sun strikes your property. Furthermore, know the kind of soil you are working with and how much nature will help with rain. Your site may have advantages; know what they are to take advantage of them. On the other hand, if there are disadvantages, know these too so you will be prepared to combat them.

PLANT HARDINESS

The hardiness zone map for plants (issued by USDA) is a universal planting guide (per minimal temperature) to what you can or cannot grow in various parts of the United States. These maps, based on average minimal night temperatures from weather stations, separate areas of the United States into zones and are very helpful in predicting the adaptability of plants to specific climates. (The zone map is included in this chapter.) Throughout this book, however, we refer to actual temperature rather than zone number to avoid confusion and constant reference to maps.

Although the zone maps are helpful, you will still need to know your own climate because temperature differences exist between hill

In the forest, woodland plants abound and should be kept and used as part of the landscape for the forest vacation house. (*Photo by Majorie Dietz*).

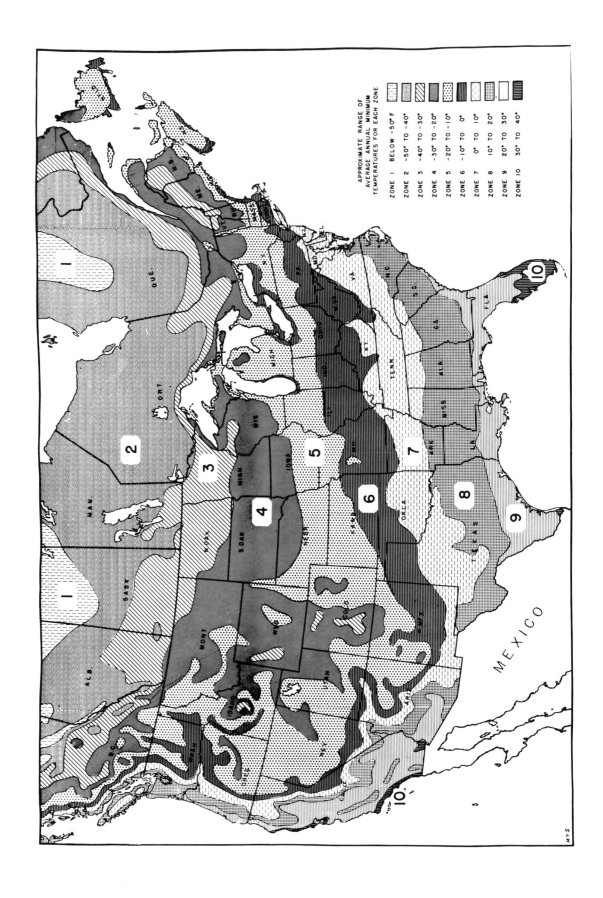

ZONE 1 BELOW -50°F
ZONE 2 -50° TO -40°
ZONE 3 -40° TO -30°
ZONE 4 -30° TO -20°
ZONE 5 -20° TO -10°
ZONE 6 -10° TO 0°
ZONE 7 0° TO 10°
ZONE 8 10° TO 20°
ZONE 9 20° TO 30°
ZONE 10 30° TO 40°

APPROXIMATE RANGE OF
AVERAGE ANNUAL MINIMUM
TEMPERATURES FOR EACH ZONE

and valley or sites along bodies of water. And thermal and fog belts are always at work. For example, there are some zones in northern California where specific conditions exist only in a small, say, 10-mile radius; temperatures may be 5 to 10 degrees lower outside this region and winds may be stronger; other different conditions may also prevail.

There are some cultural rules to help you help your plants in regard to hardiness. Do not feed plants in late summer with high nitrogen fertilizers that can force late succulent growth and reduce hardiness of many plants like roses, perennials, and broad-leaved evergreens.

Mulching (using stones or ground fir bark, peanut hulls, straw, or newspapers) keeps the soil temperature warm late in the season. Some growers keep plants mulched all year. Others apply a mulch after the soil has warmed up in spring and growth has started. If mulches are put in place too early, they stop growth because soil stays cool. In fall, apply mulches after the soil is frozen.

Some mulches are organic materials that will decay in time and add to soil improvement; others—aluminum foil for example—have to be removed.

Soil moisture is important because evergreens and deciduous trees and shrubs lose water through their stems in winter. When the ground is frozen, the plant is unable to absorb water and replenish moisture lost. Mulches help.

USDA Climate Hardiness Map.

4. Your Chosen Place

As mentioned, your vacation home may be by the sea, or in the desert, in the forest, hillside, or in a temperate region. Just what you choose depends upon your own personal tastes, and in each case gardening will entail individual planning. Just how to proceed often upsets the newcomer, but do not let it because there are plants for all geographic locations, and there are ways to garden for all kinds of people—avid gardeners and not-so-avid ones.

Naturally, any gardener will want his surroundings to be attractive and eye-appealing. This is part of the vacation theme. If you want to look at that lone locust tree surrounded by concrete outside your window, you would have stayed at home. The average vacationer wants beauty to surround him, and this can be done on a small or large scale, depending entirely upon you. There are ways to start wisely to plan your vacation landscape, ways to improve it through the years, and even ways to keep it beautiful just for a season (if you are renting). But no matter which road you take, you are going to have to know something about plants and what they can and cannot do for you in your own individual place.

By the Sea

The family that settles by the sea usually does not want to do any gardening at the start. They will be more inclined to enjoy their retreat and relax, but this is wise. However, once people are adjusted to their area and have had time to see what is there, inevitably the gardening bug will bite: by the sea the color of flower and foliage appears brighter and in shades more distinct than in many other areas.

Seaside

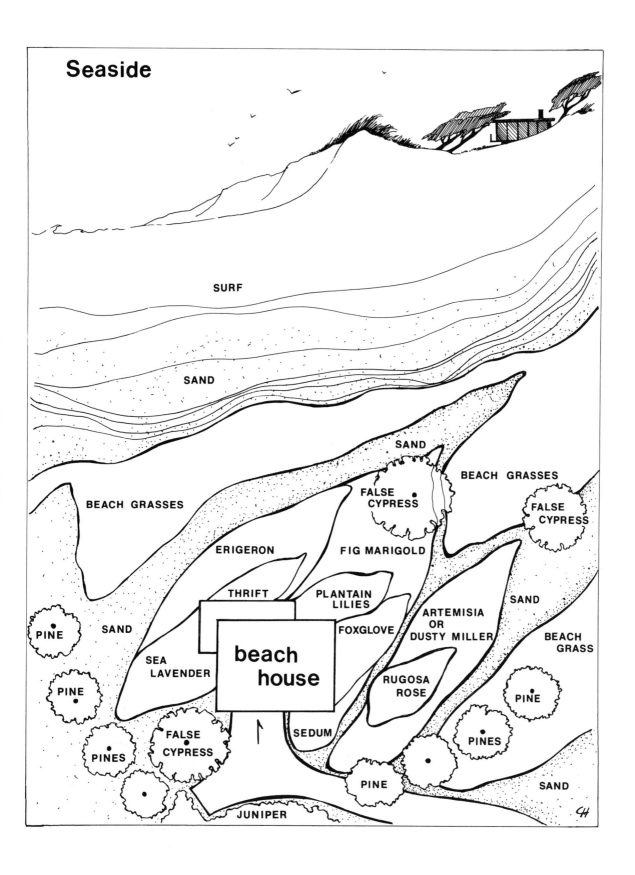

The beauty of seaside gardens is replete with wind and sand, salt spray and tides. Yet despite storms and the woeful forces of nature, and whether along the Jersey shore, down in Florida, or above the surf of the Pacific, beautiful gardens are possible. Native plants like inkberry, shadbush, and bayberry can be used successfully as well as plants from New Zealand, Australia, and China that can tolerate and thrive in windy situations. Just how you select your plants, how you place them (protection from the wind), and so forth is what makes the seaside garden a successful one. (When we talk about the sea we can mean rocky coasts or sandy dunes; each deserves special and appropriate plantings.) Each area, whether north or south, will dictate different choices of plants, too.

When you are planning your garden by the sea, select a place (if at all possible) that is somewhat protected: a cove, a natural out-cropping of rock, or an inlet area where a sand dune may offer a barrier against the wind and salt. If the terrain is such that these places do not exist, concentrate on windbreaks of various kinds to make gardening easier for you, because the wind is your main enemy.

Not yet landscaped, this vacation house by the sea calls for low shrubs to frame the house and some small trees. The existing plant material—grasses, ground cover—should be left as part of the plan. (*Photo courtesy California Redwood Assoc.*)

The first thought that usually comes to mind is fencing, but think again. Most fences, unless meticulously constructed to thwart wind, allow wind to merely scale the fence and then whip with severe force into the garden, causing more damage than a looser screen might provide.

Instead of fencing, consider natural barriers such as shrubs and trees planted thickly because they will protect an area from severe wind and at the same time take away some salt spray. Also, if on a hill, roots of sturdy plants will hold the soil.

Although there are certain plants that will withstand wind and salt spray (and these are the ones to use as your first line of defense), other and more plants can be grown where partial protection exists, and farther from the sea still other plants can survive.

The soil by the sea is liable not to be the very best, so reconditioning will be a necessity in most areas (see Chapter 2). Of course, as in all gardening, emphasize what is already there. If there are stone outcroppings or great ledges, use suitable planting to soften the scene. Place trees and shrubs where they would naturally seem to exist—next to a ledge, behind a hill, near a gully. The idea is to

A small vacation retreat uses nature as its landscaper; some native flowers have been added along the drive and a clump of shrubbery at the left to provide some scale. A simple but attractive scene. (*Photo courtesy Acorn Structures Inc.; Photographer: Sam Robbins*).

design the garden by the sea so that it is part of the total scene, not just a tacked-on afterthought.

Trees are the mainstay of a garden. However, only certain ones will tolerate the seaside position with ease. You can grow others, but they require more attention, seldom desirable unless you are an avid gardener. Actually, only a few trees are needed because beauty in the seaside garden comes from what is left out, not what is put in. A few large ones and two or three small trees are all you need to provide a framework. Once planted, the trees require little care.

There are trees for each situation, such as Australian laurel (Pittosporum), which is perfectly happy in Florida, the Gulf states, and along the Pacific. (These trees will not survive on the East Coast.) The black locust (*Robinia pseudoacacia*) can survive almost any seaside location, and poplars and willows are other good suggestions. Eucalyptus trees are well known along the West Coast, and the popular holly (Ilex genus) offers the Eastern seaboard gardener a multitude of choices. Sweet gum (*Liquidambar styraciflua*) is another good seaside tree. (For complete listing see Chapter 5.)

The above trees will offer a shower of color in spring and autumn, but for winter beauty look to the evergreens. Pines, of which there are dozens, are suitable for many seaside positions, and the lovely spruces that thrive at Bar Harbor, Maine, are robust growers against wind and salt spray. The yews (Taxus genus) are adaptable and rewarding and belong in seaside gardens; although not as tolerant of salt spray or wind, they can flourish once established.

Shrubs include an array of wonderful plants—flowering and evergreen—to give dimension to the garden. You will need more of these than trees, but the work load can be lessened by selecting those that tolerate sandy soils and those that are indigenous to shoreline habitat. Place shrubs carefully; do not use one or two here or there, but plant many of one kind in an area. A staggered arc is good landscaping because it provides dimension and depth, or use a heavy row as a barrier for lower-growing plants.

You will have to give shrubs more attention than trees. They need very good soil preparation, heavy feeding, mulching, and supporting, until roots get established. Balled and burlapped and container-grown shrubs are best for the beginner rather than bare-root material that can be difficult to get started unless constant attention is given.

Bayberry (*Myrica genus*) is a sturdy shrub, and there are many varieties that can be used in seaside gardens. These native plants act as a sand binder and as landscape material where a trim and simple look is needed. Famous for its showy white flowers and purple or red fruits, the beach plum (*Prunus maritima*) is well known along the coast of various parts of the Northeast. This is a rugged long-lived shrub that can tolerate sandy soil with abandon. Cytisus (broom) is also popular along the East and West Coasts and indeed grows so well in California that it is considered a weed. But it is an important plant for seaside gardens because when planted in groups it provides a focal point.

Cotoneasters are well suited to hot dry situations exposed to the wind; there are dozens to choose from. Pyracantha is a topnotch shrub and seems to enjoy life in almost any place. This is an excellent landscaping subject that can be used for hedges or for color in the garden. Hydrangeas and hollies are other amenable plants, with many species that will grow at seaside locations, and the lovely quince bushes seen along the Atlantic seaboard offer grand color. Not to be forgotten are junipers and grape holly, viburnum and weigelas, and, finally, splendid Rugosa roses. Heath and heather are other possibilities for the seaboard locations. (Choose plants that grow in your region; note minimum night temperatures in the Chapter 5 plant descriptions.)

In the Desert

The desert, like the sea, can be a harsh environment for plants. But even here plants do survive, and lovely gardens are possible. Once

A vacation home used most of the year needs more planting than the casual cabin or A-frame. A lawn is the focal point of this plan. Some shrubs and trees complete the setting and annuals are used for seasonal color. (*Photo by Matthew Barr*).

Desert

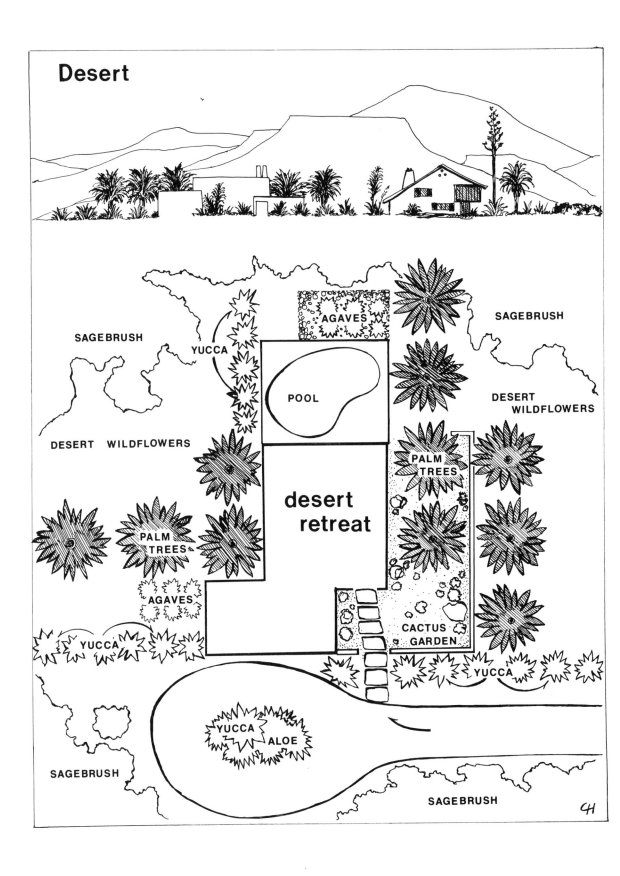

again, selection of plants is vital, and those that can tolerate drought are prime choices, if you want easy gardening and time to relax.

If you are in very desert conditions, where rainfall does not exceed 10 to 12 inches a year, you must rely on desert plants such as cacti and succulents. In most cases, however, beautiful gardens can be created in desert conditions, and there are many plants to use. The prime consideration will be improving the soil and using drought-resistant plants that can tolerate little water and do not have to be flooded constantly (see Chapter 2 for soil care).

The desert background is stark beauty, and the differences between gardening in arid regions versus other regions is soil quality, high winds, and intense sun. In such situations plants such as azaleas and camellias simply will not grow because they like acid soil and high humidity. The constant necessity of watering will not help because the irrigation defeats the aim of making soil more neutral.

You can irrigate and improve the soil to grow some plants you desperately want, but wind is another factor. There is little you can do, aside from hedges and trees, to battle the wind, but this involves a great deal of work for the vacation gardener. But where wind and soil are a problem, sun is at a premium, and the desert garden has plenty of sunlight to nourish hundreds of plants.

Generally the desert architecture is Pueblo or Spanish, small and one-storied, and often of ranch-type design. Houses such as these should not be laden with plants but be part of the landscape plan and blend well; this means low-growing plants. As at the seaside, a few trees, some shrubs, and perhaps a flower garden will make the grounds attractive and not require undue work. Native plants are helpful not only because they are accustomed to the conditions but also because they belong. They are brilliant in color and strong in line. Cacti and yucca are good landscape choices. Cottonwood, Russian olive, and weeping willow trees are also very appropriate for the adobe colors and terrain. Dogwood and roses, geraniums and hollyhocks all blend beautifully with the architecture, as do the many succulents.

Evergreens in the desert scene can become dirty trees with dusty brown foilage, but to eliminate a completely stark landscape you will need some in the winter. And they must be watered during that time because many areas of the desert have dry winters as well as other

Desert plants are used exclusively to furnish greenery and drama for this vacation home. The sand area near the house has not been cultivated but purposely left for contrasting color. (*Photo Acorn Structures Inc.; Photographer: Sam Robbins*).

dry seasons. If you only use your vacation home a few months of the year, you will have to have someone water the evergreens or they will not survive. Arbovitae, junipers, and cedars are the mainstay of the evergreen lineup, and California blue spruce and Arizona cypress can be used too for landscaping. In general, keep large shade trees away from the house, and use them as a vista instead of planting them near a window on the east or west side of the house. (Put the trees somewhat to the north to help block the intense August sun.) Flat houses (prevalent in the desert) really do not need large trees that can dwarf the house. Do not forget flowering trees, which not only give good shade but also are beautiful in the spring. And in winter the trunks of peach, redbud, flowering crab, and wisteria trees make artistic silhouettes.

Mountain ash and catalpa and some of the maples, as well as the hackberry and Russian olive, will tolerate drought and poor soils and still endure. Flowering trees like cherry, crab, and dogwoods are other equally fine candidates and are excellent landscape subjects. They are not overly large and can be used along with a few shade trees and shrubs to create a fine garden. Hawthorn and magnolias can also be tried, although they may require somewhat more care.

Shrubs cannot be dismissed in the desert garden because with vertical trees they provide mass and background. Abelia and buddleia are excellent plants for the arid gardens, and cotoneaster, which thrives almost anywhere, offer a number of varieties. Crape myrtle does exceptionally well in the southern areas, and dogwood and euonymus are valuable landscape materials for the total plan and have many uses. Hydrangeas, although needing an acid soil, can prosper in the desert site, and privet is always helpful.

If all this seems like gardening on too large a scale, consider small stone and wall, container, or patio gardens. If there is a rock formation, use it to advantage by planting rock plants and alpines in the crevices. The rocks prevent loss of moisture by evaporation and also shade the roots to keep them cool.

Another easy way to garden in the areas of heat and drought is to use paved gardens. Paving in conjunction with sparse planting and container plants creates a fine way of landscaping. It is especially useful to the vacationer who is at his place only a few months a year. Once established, the paved garden can take care of itself. The pavings, which can be concrete, tile, brick, or stone, should be used with informal plantings of juniper, heather, and creeping plants. Add a few small trees and the garden is complete with little work on your part. Beds of pachysandra mixed with brick paving in conjunction with a specimen olive tree can also make a small garden spot ideal.

Another approach for the busy person is a garden in the Japanese manner, where plantings are sparse and stones and pebbles are used to a great extent. These are low-maintenance, highly beautiful gardens. Their planning and installation may take time and money, but once established these gardens of simple and sometimes austere beauty can save weeks of work. Besides the stone and sand, mix in a few flowering trees, some lovely grasses, and individual rock groupings with plants such as mugho pine. Not much to care for, yet the complete plan creates a lovely scene.

THE TEMPERATE LANDSCAPE

If your vacation home is in temperate all-year regions such as South Carolina and Georgia, Alabama and Mississippi (southern parts), or Florida, summer weather is generally uniformly good. Winters will differ in climate between the northernmost points and the southern extremes. However, these areas are generally without great elevations and moisture throughout the years is fairly uniform. Soils will differ from one area to the next.

A garden in these regions immediately brings to mind visions of lush vegetation and verdant greenery. But this is the problem—it is a question of what *not* to grow rather than what to grow. Because of abundant moisture and abundant sun, plants grow luxuriantly, so you can become bogged down in gardening rather than enjoying it. Use a garden plan that is eye appealing but of easy maintenance. The best idea is to landscape well but with a restraining hand.

The all-year temperate garden will require more planning and planting, with a pleasing blend of trees and shrubs, small plants, and perhaps a lawn. Even with a minimum setting of, say, a dozen trees and twenty or twenty-five shrubs, pruning and maintenance will be needed, so this garden will need more work than the usual site.

The trees should be the framework for the house and the garden. They should give the shade that is necessary against hot sun and should be used as vertical accents to complement lower shrubs and perennial gardens.

Temperate landscape plan

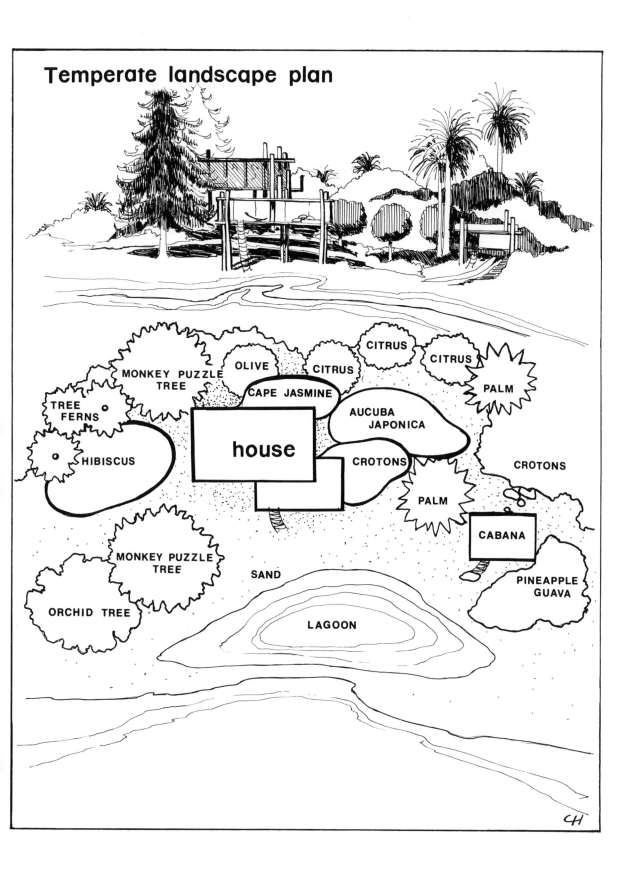

CITRUS

MONKEY PUZZLE TREE

OLIVE

CITRUS

CITRUS

PALM

TREE FERNS

CAPE JASMINE

AUCUBA JAPONICA

HIBISCUS

house

CROTONS

CROTONS

PALM

CABANA

MONKEY PUZZLE TREE

SAND

PINEAPPLE GUAVA

ORCHID TREE

LAGOON

CH

Where the weather is good all year favorite plants include a host of roses and azaleas, camellias, bamboos and other grasses too. The azalea gardens of the lower South are well known and there are no more important plants for these regions than the many species of camellias. Indeed there is plenty of material and what you use depends on the garden plant itself. Again, it is the proper selection of plants for the specific climate that makes successful gardening for the vacationer.

Close spacing of shrubs is beneficial in the seaside and desert garden but in areas of good growing conditions all year, plant shrubs with plenty of space to allow them to grow. Use them in groups: side-sweeping arcs rather than dotted here or there. Try to paint a harmonious flow of plant material by using foliage, color, texture, and mass. Concentrate on a wealth of color to make the garden beautiful to enjoy on your vacation. But at the same time (as cautioned previously) you do not want so many plants that gardening requires all your free time.

Lawns impart a lush carpet of green, and although difficult to establish and get started, lawns are not as difficult to maintain as you might expect once they are growing. They will, of course, need weeding and maintenance, but they can cover a vast amount of ground. In essence, with a good lawn only a few trees and masses of shrubs will be needed. An established lawn can make gardening easy rather than difficult. A grass area is important, but if you are at your vacation home only a few months, lawns can became a problem unless you have a monthly maintenance service (generally quite difficult to find and expensive to have these days). But ground covers such as ophiopgon, honeysuckle, and English ivy may be a better answer. In any case, a lawn or ground cover will help to minimize the expense of plant material. (See Chapter 7.)

Green is the predominant color of gardens, but be aware that there are many shades of green—blue-green, gray-green, silvery-green, and yellow-green. It is the blending of the shades of color that will make a handsome overall garden.

Cutting and flower gardens should be part of the temperate garden because plants are easy to grow and bloom profusely in these sunny areas. And they can be enjoyed only a few months of the year if that is all the time you spend at your vacation home.

With good gardening weather most of the year, there are many trees that can be used for many purposes: shade, foliage, and flowering. The decision of what to choose is entirely a matter of personal taste. Maples are prime candidates, and from the Ficus group there are many lovely trees, such as *F. benjamina* (popular as a house plant in cold climates). Magnolias can be grown with ease, as can Quercus, Catalpa, and Gingko. *Cercis canadensis* (the redbud tree) is small and an excellent landscape subject; so is *Albizzia julibrissin,* a handsome colorful tree. *Cornus florida* (dogwood) is another good subject.

Larger trees for vertical accent and planting vistas include *Platanus occidentalis, Liquidambar styraciflua,* and *Carya alba.* Evergreen trees include a host of Eucalyptus species and Ilex, as well as my favorite: *Cinnamonum camphora,* an impressive tree when rightly placed. These trees can grow to great heights and make definite statements, so use them with discretion; you want some but not too many. Use them for what they can do for the grounds rather than just as a tree to see.

In Hillside or Forest

In vacation homes on hillsides or in the forest, nature does most of the gardening for you. You can embellish the natural plantings somewhat with other plants, but basically native trees and shrubs—plants of all kinds—are the answer.

The hillside cabin is popular because of the beautiful vistas of the terrain. But such beautiful sites on slopes and hillsides—high or low—bring in some landscaping problems: Rarely is a cabin or site on a level lot.

A sloping site (hillside) may be a natural slope or a carved out "bench," with a sheer drop in front and a cut in the rear. Every slope presents a different landscaping problem, and an overall solution for all situations is impossible, but certain features are common in all hillside properties.

Although extensive landscapes and breathtaking beauty can be achieved in a hillside site, it may present an awful lot of gardening, more than the vacationer wants to tackle. Our plans and suggestions are kept simple so gardening can be done when you want to do it and not so you have to do it.

Forest

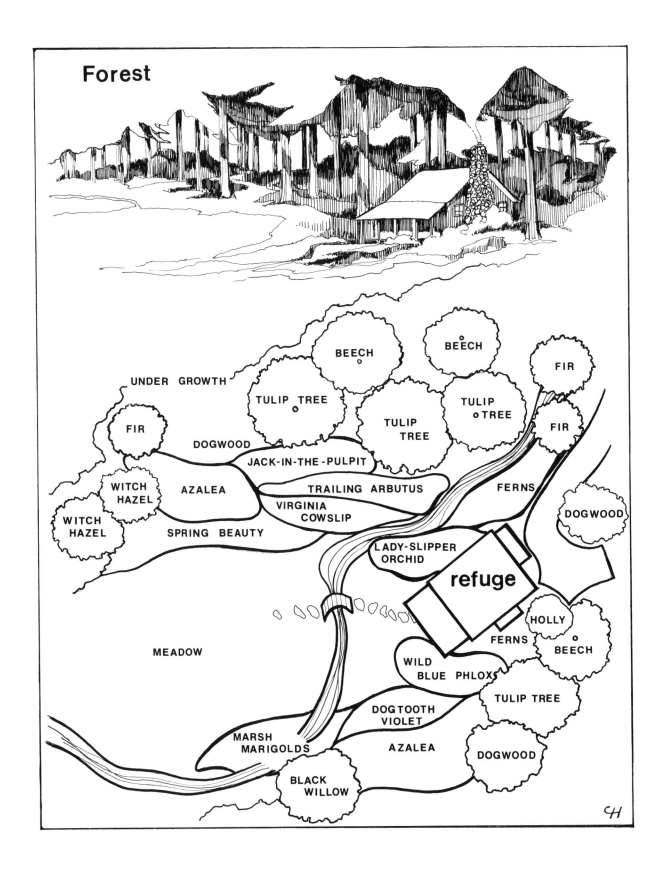

With hillside houses, the natural plant life surrounding the house is kept intact as much as possible on three sides. For example, following the slope, the house is strung out along the face of the slope. It fits into the site with a minimum of effort. Level areas for outdoor use may be scarce, so consider deck gardens. The house can also float somewhat over the slope, with a level deck extending by the rooms outside. This is a smart way of building in hilly terrains because there is little altering of the natural site and grading is not erupted, so erosion and drainage problems are minimized.

The benches carved out for hillside homes are generally in a series, and it is at the front where most landscaping should be done. This landscaping should marry the natural background with new plantings. Generally there will be trees and shrubs, so intelligent placement of new trees and shrubs can continue the flow of plant material. This, along with interesting meandering paths and walks and steps, may be all that is needed to complete the scene for easy gardening.

In the hillside home what level land there is should be used for a patio or terrace rather than for strict gardening purposes.

A small garden between the natural vegetation and the house is desirable in the hillside vacation home. Use a few well-chosen native shrubs and some ground cover; that is about all there is to it. However, each planting group should have meaning, and shrubs and low-growing trees should be used to blend into the natural scene. Where there are rocks and outcroppings, use groups of shrubs for focal points. Because most hillside retreats are on slopes, lawns are difficult if not impossible to have. But ground covers can accomplish a natural union between what is there and the clearing to the house. And ground covers are easy to maintain once in place and will not obstruct views.

Decks, frequent in hillside vacation houses, are fine places for container plants in ornamental planters. Sometimes only deck planting may be needed, in which case no garden at all will be necessary. Container gardening is easy, and almost any plant can be grown in a pot or tub, temporarily or permanently. Also, this kind of gardening allows the owner to move plants indoors when he is away. (See Chaper 7.)

The most important part of hillside gardening concerns suitable planting of paths and walks to and around the property. Where possible, do clear areas for interesting paths.

The house in the forest (woods) also relies on natural gardening, even more so than the hillside vacation spot. Native plant material is best when supplemented with some cultivated plants. Gardening in the forest is essentially gardening in shady areas. Leave what is already there—it will generally be an attractive natural setting—and enlarge on it. Add your own little secret garden, perhaps a small flower garden. This is easy gardening, but it still involves some planning, planting, and thought. If you spend only a few weeks of the year in the home, you can still have a lovely garden in a short time because most of the garden is already there for you.

What kind of garden plan should you follow in the forest? Basically create a small garden between the house and the forest. This

A redwood hideway has been simply landscaped with ferns as the dominant plant. A tree has been added at the left and the natural forest provides the serene background. (*Photo courtesy California Redwood Assoc.*)

will mean clearing and pruning and perhaps replanting. The choice
of plants for the garden will be great, but limit yourself to small
plantings and groupings to complement nature's backdrop. Do not
try to compete; plan and plant to harmonize with what is already
there. This does not rule out a garden per se but rather gives you
a creative hand to fashion an extension of what already exists.

Generally trees will already be on the property, as will shrubs
(you will have numerous shade trees and will be working mainly
with them). As with the hillside property, a clearing between the
house and the forest is necessary. This area should be planted with
low ground covers, appropriate native shrubs, and interesting paths
and walks. Maintenance of such a garden plan is minimal and can
provide a handsome effect.

Native plants, the mainstay of the forest home, should be used
to the fullest, with some cultivated perennials and annuals brought
in if time permits. If the property is solidly forested, you will have
to do some clearing and pruning to provide handsome vistas; for
example, a solid row of existing trees may be blocking a splendid
view, or shrubs that have gone without taming for years may ob-
scure other vistas, as well as cut out sun. Your major work and cost
in the forest home will be to prune and remove some (very little),
but not all the vegetation. Most likely you will want to keep the
forest as it is on three sides, but the front of the house should be
open to sky and view.

What to take out and what to leave may seem like a dilemma,
but approach it slowly, taking one area at a time. Walk through
your property to decide just how much better it might be if that
clump were removed or at least thinned. Decide where you want
paths to meander into the forest and how to plan them so they
lead to the house. Straight paths are rarely interesting; curved and
winding pathways are charming.

Small flower gardens are delightful in the woods, and here you
can grow a galaxy of wild flowers and bulbs. Once in the ground
bulbs will propagate through the years and produce colonies of
flowers for your grounds. Remember that in the forest there will
be ample leaf mold and humus for you to use. You will not be de-
pleting nature because as time evolves nature replenishes the supply
as leaves fall and natural decay goes on.

Desert cacti and low ground cover and bamboo provide a simple natural look for this patio garden of a vacation desert home. The effect is totally pleasing. Note the hedge in rear of wall for privacy. (*Photo by Gary Brant*).

Gardening with wildflowers is fun everywhere but especially rewarding in the forest. Woodland gardening offers rich soil and excellent conditions to really get things growing. And once established the plants will more or less fend for themselves.

Set woodland plants in natural groups. For example, trilliums, American columbine (*Aquilegia canadensis*), and various types of ferns always grow in colonies. Creeping phlox (*Phlox stolonifera*),

Hillside

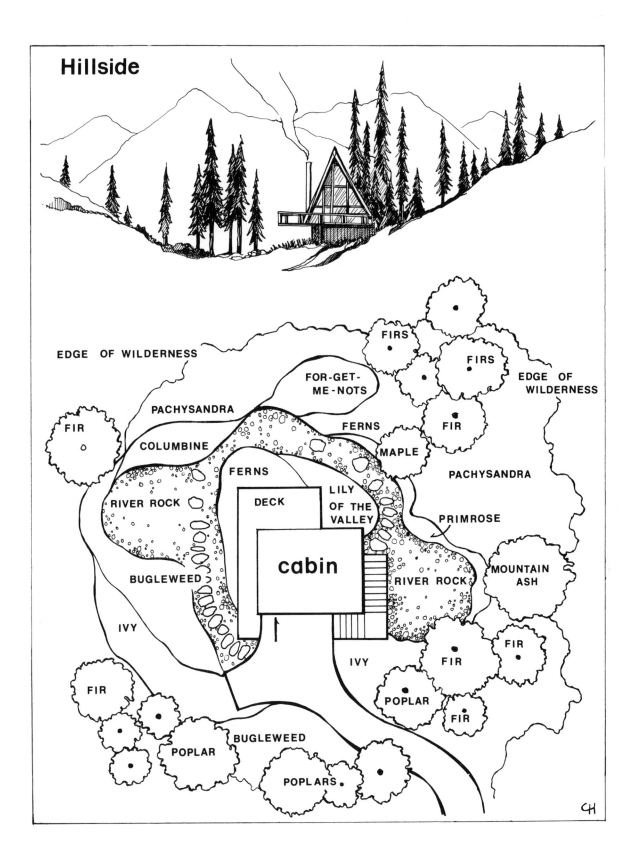

with its mauve flowers, is stunning, and the leathery green leaves of wild ginger (Asarum) are a handsome garden accent. Solomon's seal (Polygonatum), with creamy white bells in spring and handsome blue berries in fall, is another good wild plant, and under trees *Galax aphylla*, with white wands of flowers and beautiful foliage, grows like a weed.

Trees, of course, play an important part in your garden. If at all possible, never remove a tree, unless it is diseased or in irreparable shape. Prune lower branches, but always remember that filtered sunlight should strike the garden site. Remove underbrush and seedling trees, and along with wild flowers use native trees and shrubs like oak leaf hydrangea (*Hydrangea quercifolia*), native viburnums, and sweet pepperbrush (*Clethra alnifolia*). Native rhododendrons, heaths, and azaleas offer immense color and are available from several sources. The common Eastern shrub *Kalmia latifolia* (mountain laurel) grows to 10 feet, with pink to white flowers in May and June. A smaller laurel (*K. polifolia*) will also grow in the rich soil of the woodlands; the blossoms are pale to deep red.

There are dozens of beautiful azaleas (rhododendrons) that can enhance a woodland garden. In the East, *Rhododendron nudiflorum* and *R. roseum* (sometimes considered a variety of *R. nudiflorum*) are favorites, as is the fragrant and lovely swamp azalea (*R. viscosum*). The flame azalea (*R. calendulaceum*) is native to the Middle Atlantic states and extends south to Georgia and Alabama. The beautiful shell pink azalea (*R. vaseyi*) is indigenous to western North Carolina but hardy as far north as southwestern New England. The largest and perhaps best-known azalea is *R. maximum*, an upright shrub that grows to 20 feet and has evergreen leaves and whitish to pink flowers. It thrives in the Carolinas but is equally good in Pennsylvania, Vermont, New Hampshire, and Maine.

Mountain rose bay or catawba rhododendron (*R. catawbiense*) is a wild shrub of the eastern United States and has dark rose-lavender flowers in May and early June.

Some other native shrubs for woodlands are pieris, leucothoe, halesia, fothergilla, shadbush, witch hazel, wild roses, spiraea, holly grape, ceanothus, sourwood, dogwood, fringe tree, and crabapples. Berried plants include hollies, bayberry, viburnums, and snowberry. (For more plants see Chapter 5.)

5. Plants for All Places

Trees and shrubs are the mainstay of the garden, and in the following sections we review the trees and shrubs most appropriate for certain geographical areas. So whether you are by the sea or in the desert, have a cabin in the forest or hills or a vacation home in a temperate clime, here are some plants to help you get started. (Also see Chapter 7 for specific kinds of plants like vines and ground covers.)

TREES AND SHRUBS FOR SEASIDE LOCATIONS

Botanical and Common Name	Approx. Height in ft.	Minimum Night Temp.	Remarks
Acer platanoides (Norway Maple)	90	—35 to —20 F.	Grows rapidly
A. pseudoplatanus (sycamore)	90	—10 to —5 F.	Dense large-leaved tree
A. rubrum (red maple)	120	—35 to —20 F.	Best show in late spring
Ailanthus altissima (tree of heaven)	60	—20 to —10 F.	Very adaptable
Casuarina equistifolia (coast beefwood)	30	—30 to —40 F.	Grows in sandy soil
Chaenomeles japonica (Japanese quince)	3	—20 to —10 F.	Valuable ornamental shrub

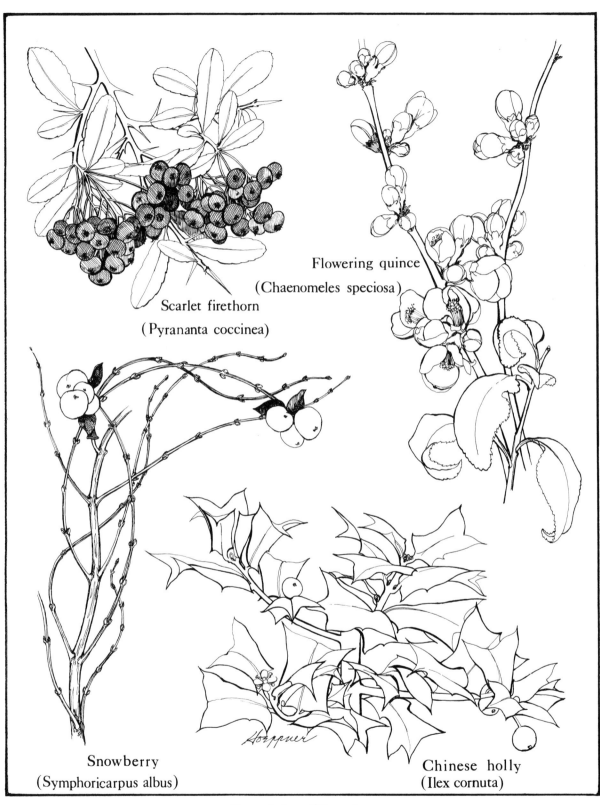

Flowering quince

(Chaenomeles speciosa)

Scarlet firethorn

(Pyrananta coccinea)

Snowberry

(Symphoricarpus albus)

Chinese holly
(Ilex cornuta)

Seaside Shrubs

Botanical and Common Name	Approx. Height in ft.	Minimum Night Temp.	Remarks
C. speciosa (flowering quince)	6	—20 to —10 F.	Many varieties
Chamaecyparis obtusa (Hinoki false cypress)	130	—20 to —10 F.	Broadly pyramidal
C. pisifera (sawara false cypress)	100	—35 to —20 F.	Many varieties
Cornus stolonifera (red Osier dogwood)	7	—50 to —35 F.	Likes moist soils
Cotoneaster dammeri (bearberry)	1	—10 to —5 F.	Good creeping shrub
C. horizontalis (rock spray)	3	—20 to —10 F.	Good for rocky areas
Crataegus phaenopyrum (Washington hawthorn)	30	—20 to —10 F.	Profuse flowers, brilliant autumn color
Cupressus macrocarpa (Monterey cypress)	75	—5 to —10 F.	Good windbreaker against view window
Cytisus canariensis (Canary Island broom)	6	—5 to 5 F.	Lovely yellow flowers
C. decumbens (prostate broom)	1	—10 to —5 F.	Good ground cover
C. kewensis (Kew broom)	1	—5 to 5 F.	Grows well on rocks
C. scoparius (Scotch broom)	1	—10 to —5 F.	Many varieties; takes abuse
Elaeagnus angustifolia (Russian olive)	20	—50 to —35 F.	Vigorous; any soil
Eucalyptus globulus compacta	200	20 to 30 F.	Another excellent windbreak tree
Fagus grandifolia (American beech)	120	—35 to —20 F.	Stellar tree
F. sylvatica (European beech)	100	—20 to —10 F.	Several varieties

Botanical and Common Name	Approx. Height in ft.	Minimum Night Temp.	Remarks
Forsythia (many kinds)	9	—20 to —10 F.	Does well in dry situations
Fraxinus americana (white ash)	120	—35 to —20 F.	Grows in almost any soil
Gleditsia triancanthos (sweet honey locust)	100	—20 to —10 F.	Several varieties
Hippophae rhamnoides (sea buckthorn)	30	—35 to —20 F.	Gray and silver foliage
Hydrangea (Many varieties)	to 15	—10 to —5 F.	Does especially well near ocean
Ilex aquifolium (English holly)	70	—5 to 5 F.	Dense, branching, pyramidal tree
I. cornuta (Chinese holly)	9	5 to 10 F.	Evergreen tree with red berries in fall
I. glabra (inkberry)	9	—35 to —20 F.	Good in very moist areas
I. opaca (American holly)	45	—10 to —5 F.	Good evergreen dense tree
I. verticillata (winterberry)	9	—35 to —20 F.	Leaves and red berries appear at same time
Juniperus chinensis sargentii (sargent juniper)	to 1	—20 to —10 F.	Excellent ground for poor soils
J. virginiana (red cedar)	90	—50 to —35 F.	Native of Eastern half of United States
Kolkwitzia amabilis (beauty bush)	10	—35 to —20 F.	Grows in hot, dry places
Laurus nobilis (laurel)	30	—5 to 5 F.	Good tough shrub
Liquidambar styraciflua (sweetgum)	140	—10 to —5 F.	Fine shape
Malus baccata (Siberian crab apple)	45	—50 to —35 F.	Lovely flowers and fruit

Botanical and Common Name	Approx. Height in ft.	Minimum Night Temp.	Remarks
M. floribunda (Japanese flowering crab apple)	30	—20 to —10 F.	Handsome foliage and flowers
Myrica californica (California bayberry)	30	5 to 10 F.	Evergreen leaves; colorful berries
M. pensylvanica (bayberry)	9	—50 to —35 F.	Does well in poor sandy soils
Picea glauca (white spruce)	90	—50 to —35 F.	Can take heat and drought
Pinus banksiana (Jack pine)	75	—50 to —35 F.	Does well on dry sandy banks
P. contorta (shore pine)	30	5 to 10 F.	Can take wet or dry soil
P. mugo mughus (Mugho pine)	4	—50 to —35 F.	Takes gravelly soil
P. nigra (Austrian pine)	90	—20 to —10 F.	Fast-growing tree
P. radidata (Monterey pine)	60	5 to 10 F.	Excellent for seaside planting
P. thunbergana (Japanese black pine)	90	—20 to —10 F.	Dense-spreading tree
Populus alba (white poplar)	90	—35 to —20 F.	Wide-spreading tree
Prunus maritima (beach plum)	6	—35 to —20 F.	Especially good for seashore planting
Pyracantha coccinea (scarlet firethorn)	6	—5 to 5 F.	Always beautiful
Quercus alba (white oak)	80	—20 to —10 F.	Needs room to grow
Q. agrifolia (California live oak)	90	20 to 30 F.	Native to California coast
Q. virginiana (live oak)	60	5 to 10 F.	Can take abuse
Robinia pseudoacacia (black locust)	80	—35 to —20 F.	Fine, late spring flowers

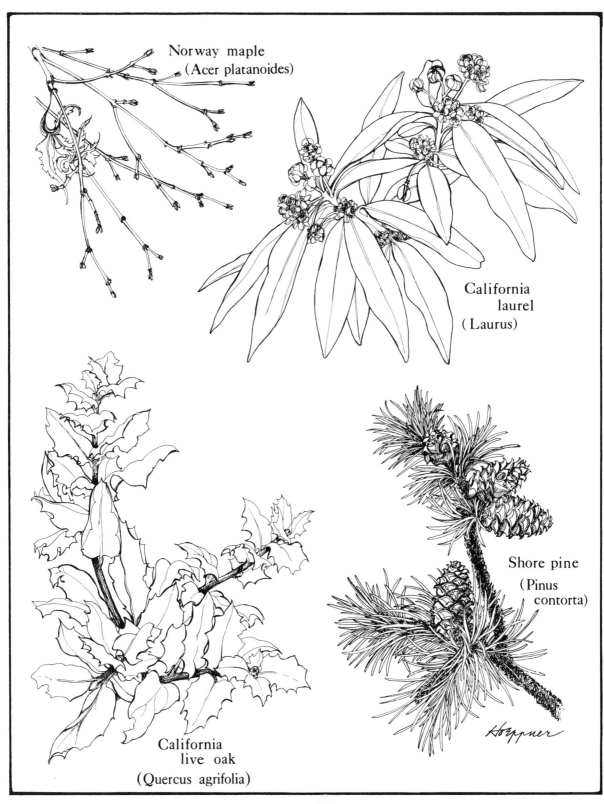

Norway maple
(Acer platanoides)

California
laurel
(Laurus)

California
live oak
(Quercus agrifolia)

Shore pine
(Pinus
contorta)

Hoppner

Seaside Trees

Botanical and Common Name	Approx. Height in ft.	Minimum Night Temp.	Remarks
Rosa rugosa (Rugosa rose)	to 1	—35 to —20 F.	Splendid along seacoast
Salix discolor (willow)	20	—35 to —20 F.	Grows in any soil
Sorbus aucuparia (mountain ash)	45	—35 to —20 F.	Red autumn color
Symphoricarpos albus laevigatus (snowberry)	6	—35 to —20 F.	Arching branches; white berries
S. orbiculatus (coralberry)	4	—50 to —35 F.	Excellent for bank planting
Syringa amurensis japonica (Japanese tree lilac)	15	—20 to —10 F.	Good for hot dry places
Tamarix pentandra	15	—50 to —35 F.	Excellent for seashore plantings
Taxus cuspidata 'Capitata' (Japanese yew)	50	—20 to —10 F.	Good landscape tree
Tilia cordata (small-leaved linden)	60	—35 to —20 F.	Dense habit
Umbellularia californica (California laurel)	75	5 to 10 F.	Favorite West Coast tree
Vaccinium corymbosum (blueberry)	12	—35 to —20 F.	Good ornamental plant
Viburnum dentatum (arrowwood)	15	—50 to —35 F.	Grows well almost any place
V. lantana (wayfaring tree)	15	—35 to —20 F.	Good plant for dry soil
V. sieboldii	30	—20 to —10 F.	Nice graceful plant
V. wrightii	9	—10 to —5 F.	Good fall colors
Weigela (many kinds)	to 10	—10 to —5 F.	Brightly colored flowers

Trees and Shrubs for Desert Regions

Botanical and Common Name	Approx. Height in ft.	Minimum Night Temp.	Remarks
Abelia floribunda	6	10 to 20 F.	Nice evergreen shrub
Acer ginnala (Amur maple)	20	—50 to —35 F.	Red fall color
A. platanoides (Norway maple)	90	—35 to —20 F.	Grows rapidly
Ailanthus altissima (tree of heaven)	60	—20 to —10 F.	Very adaptable
Albizzia julibrissin (silk tree)	20	5 to 10 F.	Very ornamental
Berberis mentorensis (mentor barberry)	7	—10 to —5 F.	Can take hot dry summers
B. stenophylla (Rosemary barberry)	9	—10 to —5 F.	Very graceful evergreen shrub
Betula davurica (Dahurian birch)	60	—20 to —10 F.	Can thrive in dry gravelly soil
B. papyrifera (canoe birch)	90	—50 to —35 F.	Stellar ornamental
B. pendula (European birch)	60	—40 to —30 F.	Graceful, but short-lived
B. populifolia (gray birch)	40	—20 to —10 F.	Yellow color in autumn
Broussonetia papyrifera (common paper mulberry)	48	—5 to 5 F.	Likes gravelly soil
Buddleia alternifolia (fountain buddleia)	12	—10 to —5 F.	Vigorous shrub
Caragana arborescens (Siberian pea shrub)	18	—50 to —35 F.	Good windbreak shrub
Catalpa speciosa (northern catalpa)	90	—20 to —10 F.	Can take heat and dryness
Cedrus atlantica (atlas cedar)	100	—5 to 5 F.	Nice pyramid

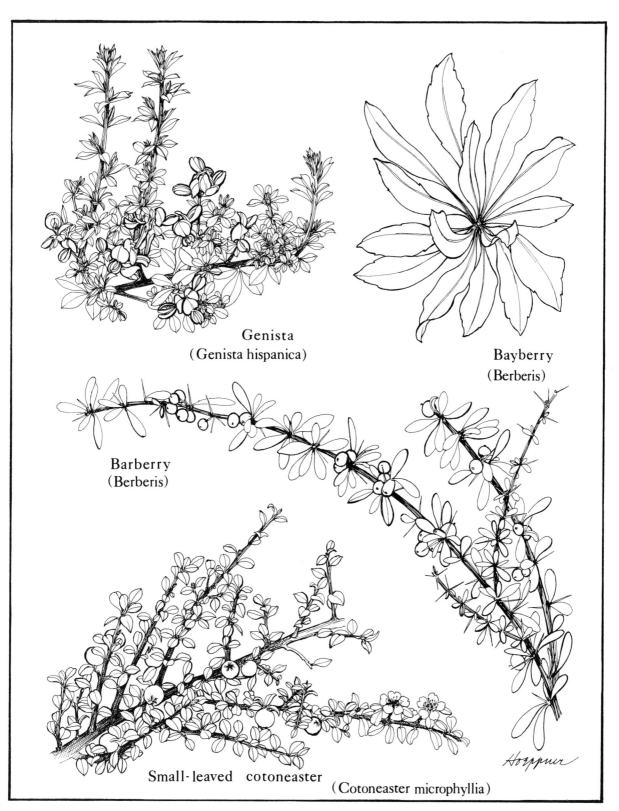

Genista
(Genista hispanica)

Bayberry
(Berberis)

Barberry
(Berberis)

Small-leaved cotoneaster (Cotoneaster microphyllia)

Desert Shrubs

Botanical and Common Name	Approx. Height in ft.	Minimum Night Temp.	Remarks
Celtis occidentalis (hackberry)	75	—50 to —35 F.	Good shade tree
Cercis canadensis (eastern redbud)	25	—20 to —10 F.	Lovely flowers
Cladrastis lutea (yellow wood)	50	—35 to —20 F.	Good specimen tree
Comptona peregrina (sweetbush)	4	—50 to —35 F.	Fernlike leaves; good natural plant
Cotinus coggygria (European smoke tree)	15	—5 to 5 F.	Lovely foliage; takes dry soil
Cotoneaster conspicua (wintergreen cotoneaster)	3	—5 to 5 F.	Good evergreen shrub for covering banks
C. dammeri (bearberry cotoneaster)	1	—10 to —5 F.	Excellent ever-green ground cover for rocky areas
C. microphylla (small-leaved cotoneaster)	3	—10 to —5 F.	A good robust plant
Crataegus oxyacantha (English hawthorn)	20	—20 to —10 F.	Pink to red flowers
C. phaenopyrum (Washington hawthorn)	30	—20 to —10 F.	Profuse flowers, brilliant autumn color
Cytisus kewensis (Kew broom)	1	—5 to 5 F.	Grows well in dry soil
C. scoparius (Scotch broom)	1	—10 to 5 F.	Many varieties
Deutzia scabra	8	—10 to —5 F.	Lovely flowering shrub
Eleagnus angustifolia (Russian olive)	20	—50 to —35 F.	Vigorous; any soil
Euonymus americanis	7	—5 to 5 F.	Good native shrub
Fraxinus pensylvanica lanceolata (green ash)	20	—50 to —35 F.	Vigorous well-shaped tree

Botanical and Common Name	Approx. Height in ft.	Minimum Night Temp.	Remarks
Gaylussacia brachycera (box huckleberry)	2	—10 to —5 F.	Good for rocky dry situations
Genista hispanica	1	—5 to 5 F.	Needs dry soil to prosper
G. tinctoria (dyers greenwood)	3	—50 to —35 F.	Needs a hot sunny spot
Ginko biloba (maidenhair tree)	120	—20 to —10 F.	Popular one
Gleditsia triacanthos (sweet honey locust)	100	—20 to —10 F.	Several varieties
Gymnocladus dioicus (Kentucky coffee tree)	90	—20 to —10 F.	Good for winter color
Hydrangea arborescens (wild hydrangea)	10	—20 to —10 F.	Excellent native
Juniperus chinensis (Chinese juniper)	60	—20 to —10 F.	Many varieties
J. scopulorum (Colorado red cedar)	36	—10 to —5 F.	Good robust tree
J. virginiana (eastern red cedar)	30–50	—50 to —35 F.	Slow growing
Koelreuteria paniculata (goldenrain tree)	30	—10 to —5 F.	Magnificent summer bloom
Laburnum waterei (golden-chain tree)	25	—10 to —5 F.	Deep yellow flowers
Lagerstromevia indica (crape myrtle)	20	5 to 10 F.	Profuse summer bloom
Leiophyllum buxifolium (sand myrtle)	2	—10 to —5 F.	Needs acid soil to prosper
Ligustrum lucidum (glossy privet)	30	5 to 10 F.	Blue-black berries
Maclura pomifera (osage orange)	60	—10 to —5 F.	Good windbreaker
Morus alba (white mulberry)	45	—20 to —10 F.	Grows fast even in gravel

Botanical and Common Name	Approx. Height in ft.	Minimum Night Temp.	Remarks
Myrica californica (California bayberry)	30	5 to 10 F.	Evergreen leaves; colorful berries
M. pensylvanica (bayberry)	9	—50 to —35 F.	Does well in poor sandy soil
Phellodendron amurense (cork tree)	50	—35 to —20 F.	Massive branches; wide open habit
Philadelphus coronarius (mock orange)	9	—20 to —10 F.	Good for dry places
Picea abies (Norway spruce)	150	—50 to —35 F.	Grows fast
P. glauca densata (black hills spruce)	90	—50 to —35 F.	Can take heat and drought
Pinus banksiana (scrub pine)	75	—50 to —35 F.	Does well on sandy banks
P. cembra (Swiss stone pine)	75	—50 to —35 F.	Slow-growing tough pine
P. nigra (Austrian pine)	90	—20 to —10 F.	Fast-growing tree
P. parviflora (Japanese white pine)	90	—10 to —5 F.	Good ornamental tree
P. rigida (pitch pine)	75	—20 to —10 F.	Picturesque tree
Platanus acerifolia (plane tree)	100	—10 to —5 F.	Popular street tree
Populus alba (white poplar)	90	—35 to —20 F.	Wide-spreading tree
Prunus amygdalus (almond)	25	5 to 5 F.	Handsome pink flowers
P. serotina (black cherry)	100	—20 to —10 F.	Handsome foliage; many varieties, some evergreen
P. serrulata (Japanese cherry)	25	—10 to 0 F.	Low grower; many kinds, some evergreen

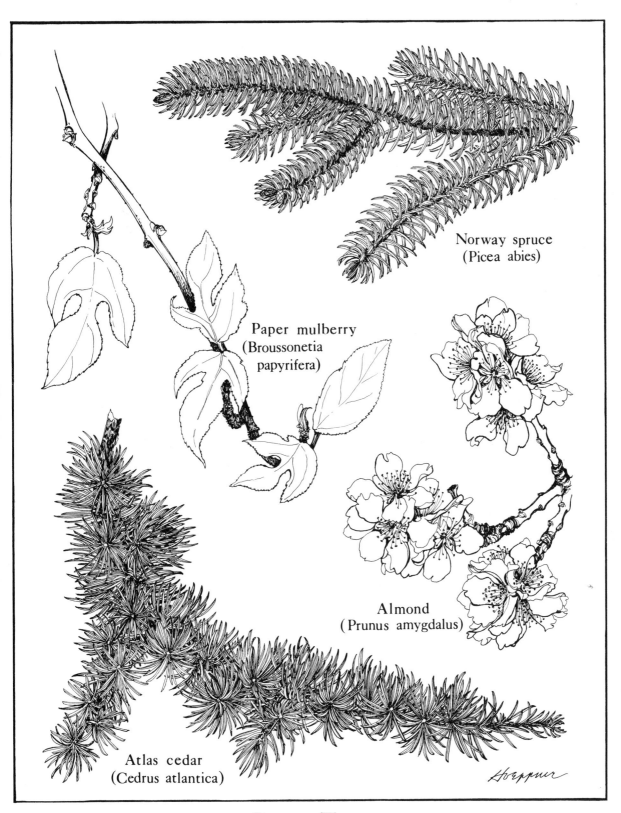

Norway spruce
(Picea abies)

Paper mulberry
(Broussonetia
papyrifera)

Almond
(Prunus amygdalus)

Atlas cedar
(Cedrus atlantica)

Hoeppner

Desert Trees

Botanical and Common Name	Approx. Height in ft.	Minimum Night Temp.	Remarks
Quercus alba (white oak)	80	—20 to —10 F.	Needs room to grow
Quercus palustris (pin oak)	120	—20 to —10 F.	Beautiful pyramid
Q. rubra (red oak)	80	—35 to —20 F.	Oval round-top tree
Rhamnus davurica (Dahurian buckthorn)	30	—50 to —35 F.	A vigorous shrub
Rhus glabra (smooth sumac)	15	—50 to —35 F.	Bright autumn color
Robinia hispida (rose acacia)	3	—10 to —5 F.	Excellent for dry soils
Robinia pseudoacacia (black locust)	80	—35 to —20 F.	Fine, late spring flowers
Rosa hugonis (Father Hugo rose)	7	—10 to —5 F.	Another excellent rose for dry soil
R. rugosa (rugosa rose)	6	—50 to —35 F.	Grows with ease
Rosmerinus officinales (rosemary)	6	—5 to 5 F.	Best in dry sandy soil
R. virginiana (Virginia rose)	6	—35 to —20 F.	Brilliant autumn foliage
Salix discolor (pussy willow)	20	—35 to —20 F.	Grows in any soil
Shepherdia canadensis (buffalo berry)	7	—50 to —30 F.	Good for poor soils
S. canadensis (russet buffalo berry)	7	—50 to —35 F.	Likes dry poor soil
Sophora japonica (Japanese pagoda tree)	60	—20 to —10 F.	Good shade tree
Sorbus aucuparia (mountain ash)	45	—35 to —20 F.	Red autumn color
Symphoricarpos albus (snowberry)	6	—35 to —20 F.	Large white berries in fall

S. orbiculatus (coralberry)	3–6	—50 to —35 F.	Spreads easily; good for dry banks
Taxus baccata (English yew)	60	—5 to 5 F.	Tough, good tree
T. cuspidata (Japanese yew)	50	—35 to —20 F.	One of the best narrow-leaved evergreens
Thuja orientalis (oriental arborvitae)	50	—5 to 5 F.	Good for hot dry locations
Tilia cordata (small-leaved linden)	60	—35 to —20 F.	Dense habit
Ulmus parvifolia (Chinese elm)	50	—10 to —5 F.	Beautiful tree
Zelkova serrata (Japanese zelkova)	90	—10 to —5 F.	Grows fast
Yucca filamentosa	3	—20 to —10 F.	Thrives in hot dry areas

TREES AND SHRUBS FOR TEMPERATE AREAS

Botanical and Common Name	Approx. Height in ft.	Minimum Night Temp.	Remarks
Abelia floribunda	6	10 to 20 F.	Nice evergreen shrub
Acacia longifolia	20	30 to 40 F.	Evergreen tree that likes dry soil
Albizzia julibrissin (silk tree)	20	5 to 10 F.	Very ornamental
Allamanda nerifolia	10	30 to 40 F.	Lovely flowering shrub
Araucaria araucana (monkey puzzle tree)	90	5 to 10 F.	Beautiful form
Arbutus menziesii	75	5 to 10 F.	Glossy green evergreen tree

Botanical and Common Name	Approx. Height in ft.	Minimum Night Temp.		Remarks
Arbutus unedo (strawberry tree)	25	10 to	20 F.	Evergreen shrub with good fall color
Ardinsia crispa (coral ardisia)	1	20 to	30 F.	Bright red berries
Arundinaria (bamboo)	15	5 to	10 F.	Many good ones
Aucuba japonica (Japanese aucuba)	15	5 to	10 F.	Fine evergreen shrub
Azalea (rhododendron)	9–15	—5 to (depending on variety)	30 F.	Many fine plants including natives; especially good are the Kurume and Indian azalea varieties
Azara lanceolata	20	20 to	30 F.	Evergreen shrub for shade
Bauhinia blakeana (orchid tree)	20	30 to	40 F.	Covered with flowers for 4 months
Broussanetia papyrifera (paper mulberry)	48	—5 to	5 F.	Dense round-headed tree
Buddleia alternifolia (fountain buddleia)	12	—10 to	—5 F.	Vigorous-growing shrub
Camellia japonica	45	5 to	10 F.	Many, many varieties; excellent
C. sasanqua	20	5 to	10 F.	Many, many varieties; excellent
Carpenteria californica (mock orange)	8	10 to	20 F.	Showy evergreen shrub
Carrisa grandiflora (natal plum)	18	20 to	30 F.	Evergreen branched shrub
Carya illinoinensis (pecan)	150	—10 to	—5 F.	Sturdy native American trees
Cassia corymobosa (flowering sensa)	10	20 to	30 F.	Free-flowering shrub

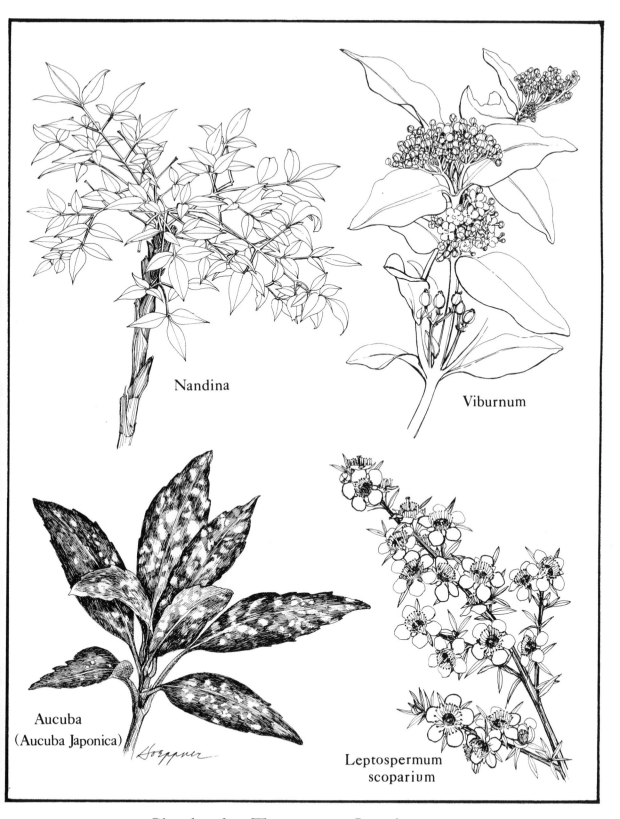

Nandina

Viburnum

Aucuba
(Aucuba Japonica)

Hoeppner

Leptospermum
scoparium

Shrubs for Temperate Landscape

Botanical and Common Name	Approx. Height in ft.	Minimum Night Temp.		Remarks
Ceanothus thyrsiflorus (blue blossom)	30	10 to	20 F.	Evergreen shrub for dry soils
Cedrus altlantica (atlas cedar)	120	—5 to	5 F.	Favorite evergreen tree
C. deodora (deodar cedar)	150	5 to	10 F.	Graceful pyramidal evergreen
Cercis canadensis (eastern redbud)	40	—10 to	—5 F.	Lovely flowers
Chamaecyparis pisifera filifera (false-cedar)	150	5 to	10 F.	Pyramidal evergreen
Cinnamonum camphora (camphor tree)	40	20 to	30 F.	Very dense evergreen tree
Citrus (many kinds)	20 to 30	30 to	40 F.	Always desirable for deep south
Clethra arborea (lily-of-the-valley; clethra)	25	20 to	30 F.	Nice autumn color
Cornus florida (flowering dogwood)	40	—20 to	—10 F.	Lovely flowering tree
Crataegus (hawthorn)	20 to 40	—20 to	—10 F.	Many fine trees with excellent color
Delonix regia (royal ponciana)	40	20 to	40 F.	Fernlike foliage lovely flowers
Deutzia scabra (snowflake deutzia)	8	—10 to	—5 F.	Many fine varieties
Elaegnus pungens (thorny elaegnus)	12	5 to	10 F.	Popular evergreen shrub
Erica mediterranea (Mediterranean heath)	5	20 to	30 F.	Evergreen shrub with needlelike leaves
Eriobotyra japonica (loquat)	20	5 to	10 F.	Needs well-drained soil and good sun
Eucalyptus camadulensis	70	20 to	30 F.	Fast-growing spreading tree

Botanical and Common Name	Approx. Height in ft.	Minimum Night Temp.		Remarks
E. viminalis	100	20 to	30 F.	Good tree for poor soil
Eugenia uniflora (surinam cherry)	25	30 to	40 F.	Good glossy evergreen
Feijoa sellowiana	18	20 to	30 F.	Dense gray foliage
Ficus macrophylla	25	30 to	40 F.	Glossy evergreen tree
Franklinia alatamaha	30	—10 to	—5 F.	Good tree for autumn color
Gardenia jasminoides (cape jasmine)	6	20 to	30 F.	Fine white flowers
Gingko biloba	120	—20 to	—10 F.	Popular, easy-to-grow tree
Gordonia lasianthus (loblolly bay)	60	10 to	20 F.	Evergreen glossy-leaved tree
Grevillea robusta (silk oak grevillea)	150	30 to	40 F.	Does well in sandy soil
Hibiscus rosa sinensis (Chinese hibiscus)	30	30 to	40 F.	Fast-growing shrub with glossy leaves
Hymenosporum flavum (sweet shade tree)	50	30 to	40 F.	Rapidly growing evergreen tree
Ilex (holly)	9	5 to	10 F.	Bright red-berried shrub; many varieties
Jacaranda acutifolia	50	30 to	40 F.	Lacy lovely tree
Jasminum officinalis	to 30	5 to	10 F.	Lovely attractive shrub
J. mesnyi	to 10	10 to	20 F.	Fine flowing vine
Juniperus chinensis (Chinese juniper)	1 to 12	—20 to	—30 F.	Evergreen pointed leaves
J. Virginiana (Eastern red cedar)	2 to 15	—50 to	—35 F.	Evergreen shrubs

Botanical and Common Name	Approx. Height in ft.	Minimum Night Temp.		Remarks
Koelreuteria formosana (Chinese flame tree)	30	20 to	30 F.	Flat-topped, easy-to-grow tree
Lagerstromeria indica (crape myrtle)	20	5 to	10 F.	Profuse summer bloom
Leptospermum laevigatum (Australia tea tree)	25	20 to	30 F.	Evergreen tree for poor soil
Ligustrum japonica (Japanese privet)	9 to 18	5 to	10 F.	Fine evergreen shrub
L. lucidum (glossy privet)	30	5 to	10 F.	Blue-back berries
L. sinense (Chinese privet)	12	5 to	10 F.	Graceful hand-some shrub
Liquidambar formosana (sweetgum)	120	5 to	10 F.	Good autumn color
Liriodendron tulipifera (tulip tree)	150	—20 to	—10 F.	Pyramidal massive tree
Macadamia ternifolia (Queensland nut)	35	30 to	40 F.	Slow-growing evergreen for deep south
Magnolia grandiflora (bull bay)	90	5 to	10 F.	Pyramidal popular tree
Magnolia virginiana (sweetbay magnolia)	60	—10 to	—5 F.	Big and waxy white flowers
Mandevilla suavolens	to 20	20 to	30 F.	Pretty flowering vine
Melia azedarach (chinaberry tree)	45	5 to	10 F.	Round-headed branching tree
Myrica californica (California bayberry)	30	5 to	10 F.	Slender upright shrub
Myrtus communis (myrtle)	to 10	20 to	30 F.	Good shrub for hot dry places
Nandina domestica	8	5 to	10 F.	An overlooked pretty plant
Nerium oleander	20	10 to	20 F.	Withstands hot dry conditions

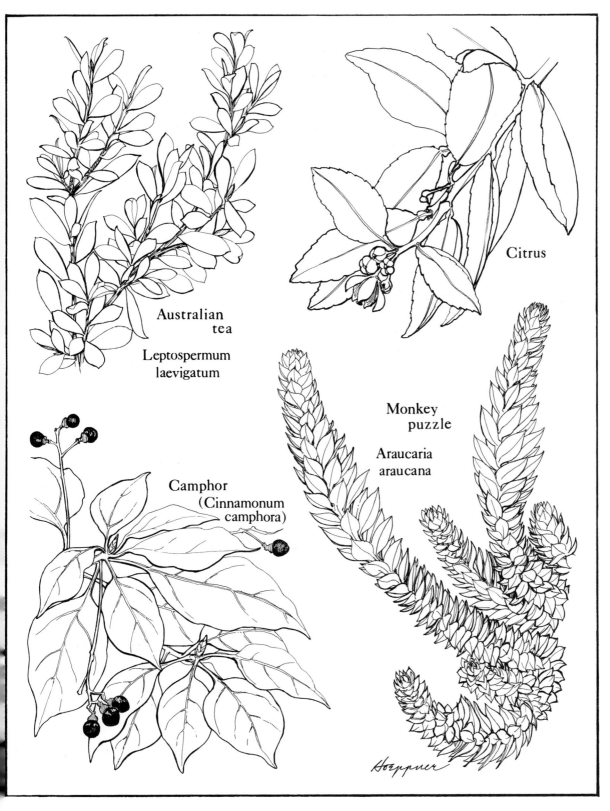

Australian
tea

Leptospermum
laevigatum

Citrus

Monkey
puzzle

Araucaria
araucana

Camphor
(Cinnamonum
camphora)

Hoeppner

Trees for Temperate Landscape

Botanical and Common Name	Approx. Height in ft.	Minimum Night Temp.		Remarks
Nyssa sinensis (Chinese sour gum)	to 50	5 to	10 F.	Outstanding autumn color
Olea europea (common olive)	25	20 to	30 F.	Good evergreen for dry soil
Osmanthus fortunei (osmanthus)	12	10 to	20 F.	A vigorous shrub; excellent in South
Oxydendrum arboreum (sorrel tree)	75	—10 to	—5 F.	Superior ornamental tree
Paulownia tomentosa (empress tree)	45	—10 to	—5 F.	Rapidly growing dense tree
Philadelphus coronarius (sweet mock-orange)	9	—20 to	—10 F.	Especially fragrant and good for dry soils
Photinia serrulata (Chinese photinia)	36	5 to	10 F.	Lovely evergreen
Phyllustachys (bamboo)	20–50	5 to	10 F.	Some lovely plants
Pinus canariense (Canary pine)	80	10 to	20 F.	Picturesque round-headed tree
Pistacia chinensis (Chinese pistache)	50	20 to	30 F.	Good Florida tree
Poncirus trifoliata (hardy orange)	35	10 to	20 F.	Good hedge in South
Pinus contorta (slash pine)	30	5 to	10 F.	Easy to grow evergreen tree
P. helepensis (Aleppo pine)	60	20 to	30 F.	Round-top evergreen pine
Pistacia chinensis (Chinese pistache)	50	20 to	30 F.	Fine autumn color
Pittosporum eugenioides	40	30 to	40 F.	Fine evergreen shrub
Platanus orientalis (oriental plane tree)	90	—5 to	5 F.	Maplelike foliage
Plumbago capensis	10	20 to	30 F.	Profuse blue flowers

Botanical and Common Name	Approx. Height in ft.	Minimum Night Temp.		Remarks
Podocarpus elongatus	70	30 to	40 F.	Good leafy shrub
P. macrophylla (yew podocarpus)	60	5 to	10 F.	Dense good yew
Pruns caroliana (Caroline cherry laurel)	40	10 to	20 F.	Glossy green evergreen tree many species
Pyracantha coccinea (firethorn)	6	—5 to	5 F.	Bright red berries
Quercus agrifolia (California live oak)	90	20 to	30 F.	Hollylike evergreen tree
G. virginiana	60	5 to	10 F.	Wide-spreading evergreen tree
Rosa (rose)	1–3	—5 to (depending on variety)	30 F.	Tea, hybrid and climbers; excellent
Roystonea regia (royal palm)	70	30 to	40 F.	Graceful palm
Schinus terebinthifolius (Brazil pepper tree)	40	30 to	40 F.	Grows easily in Southern Florida
Spirea prunifolia	9	—20 to	—10 F.	Double white flowers
S. thunbergeri	5	—20 to	—10 F.	Feathery shrub
Thuja occidentalis (American arborvita)	60	—50 to	—35 F.	Popular evergreen tree
Vaccinum arboreum	10	5 to	10 F.	Evergreen shrub
V. ovatum (box blueberry)	10	5 to	10 F.	Evergreen shrub
Viburnum odoratissima	10	10 to	20 F.	Fine evergreen shrub
Weigela (many species)	to 10	—10 to	—5 F.	Brightly colored flowers

TREES AND SHRUBS FOR FOREST AND HILLSIDE

Botanical and Common Name	Approx. Height in ft.	Minimum Night Temp.	Remarks
Abies balsamea (balsam fir)	50	—35 to —20 F.	Handsome and ornamental
A. concolor (white fir)	120	—20 to —10 F.	Landscape tree
Acer rubrum (red maple)	120	—35 to —20 F.	Best show in late spring
A. saccharum (sugar maple)	120	—35 to —20 F.	Many varieties
Aesculus glabra (Ohio buckeye)	30	—35 to —20 F.	Autumn colors
A. parviflora (bottle brush buckeye)	12	—10 to —5 F.	Good small tree
Amelanchier canadensis (serviceberry)	60	—20 to —10 F.	Tough robust tree
Andromeda polifolia (bog rosemary)	21	—50 to —35 F.	Fine shrub
Aronia arbutifolia (red chokeberry)	10	—20 to —10 F.	Good colorful shrub
Betula papyrifera (white birch)	100	—50 to —35 F.	Fine ornamental
Calycanthus floridus (Carolina allspice)	10	—20 to —10 F.	Dense shrub with glossy foliage
Carya glabra (pignut)	40	—20 to —10 F.	Grows slowly
C. ovata (shagbark hickory)	120	—20 to —10 F.	Narrow upright habit
Ceanothus americanus (New Jersey tea)	3	—20 to —10 F.	Does fine in poor soil
Cephalanthus occidentalis (buttonball bush)	20	—20 to —10 F.	A shrub for moist soils
Cercis canadensis (eastern redbud)	40	—10 to —5 F.	Lovely flowers

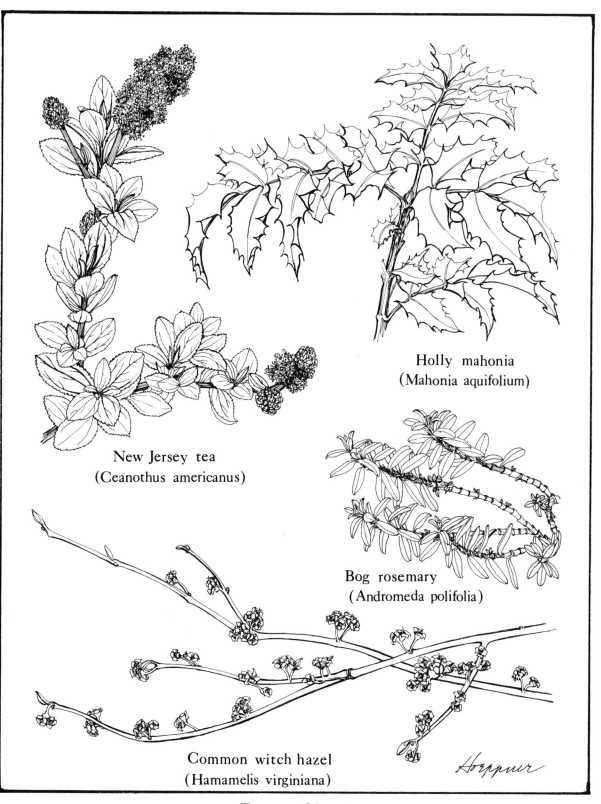

Holly mahonia
(Mahonia aquifolium)

New Jersey tea
(Ceanothus americanus)

Bog rosemary
(Andromeda polifolia)

Common witch hazel
(Hamamelis virginiana)

Forest Shrubs

Botanical and Common Name	Approx. Height in ft.	Minimum Night Temp.	Remarks
Chamaecyparis lawsoniana (lawson false cypress)	120	—10 to —5 F.	Good evergreen
Chioanthus virginica (fringetree)	30	—20 to —10 F.	For flowers
Cladrastis lutea (yellowwood)	50	—35 to —20 F.	Fine tree for flowers and foliage
Clethra alnifolia (summersweet clethra)	10	—30 to —20 F.	Good tough shrub
Cornus amomum (silky dogwood)	8	—30 to —20 F.	Good red autumn color
Cornus florida (flowering dogwood)	40	—20 to —10 F.	Stellar, ornamental
C. stolonifera (red osier dogwood)	10	—50 to —35 F.	Good color
Corylus americana (American hazelnut)	10	—20 to —10 F.	Nicely shaped ornamental tree
Crataegus nitida (glossy hawthorn)	30	—20 to —10 F.	Fruits all winter
C. phaenopyrum (Washington hawthorn)	30	—20 to —10 F.	Brilliant autumn color
Diospyros virginiana (common persimmon)	75	—20 to —10 F.	Canopy habit
Elaegnus commutata (silverberry)	12	—50 to —35 F.	Fine hardy shrub
Euonymus americanus (strawberry bush)	6	—50 to —35 F.	Shrub with good autumn color
Fagus grandifolia (American beech)	90	—35 to —20 F.	Popular tree
Fothergilla gardenii (dwarf fothergilla)	3	—10 to —5 F.	Good small bush
Franklinia alatamaha (franklinia)	30	—10 to —5 F.	Red foliage in autumn
Fraxinus pennsylvanica (red ash)	60	—50 to —35 F.	Yellow autumn color

Botanical and Common Name	Approx. Height in ft.	Minimum Night Temp.	Remarks
Gaylussacia brachycera (box huckleberry)	2	—10 to —5 F.	Good small evergreen
Gleditsia triancanthos (honey locust)	140	—20 to —10 F.	Many varieties
Gymnocladus diocius (Kentucky coffee tree)	100	—20 to —10 F.	Nice open habit
Halesia carolina (Carolina silverbell)	40	—10 to —5 F.	Tree with good autumn color
H. monticola (mountain silverbell)	100	—10 to —5 F.	Large-flowered tree
Hamamelis vernalis (spring witch hazel)	10	—10 to —5 F.	Blooms in early spring
H. virginiana (common witch hazel)	15	—10 to —5 F.	Shrub bears flowers in late fall
Hydrangea arborescens (wild hydrangea)	10	—20 to —10 F.	Dense upright shrub
H. quercifolia (oakleaf hydrangea)	6	—10 to —5 F.	Handsome shrub with oak-shaped leaves
Ilex glabra (inkberry)	9	—35 to —20 F.	Willowy good shrub
I. opaca (American holly)	50	—10 to —5 F.	Needs well-drained soil
I. verticillata (winterberry)	10	—35 to —20 F.	Shrub with good winter color
Itea virginica (sweet spire)	10	—10 to —5 F.	Pretty native shrub
Juniperus virginiana (red cedar)	100	—50 to —35 F.	Slow growing
Kalmia latifolia (mountain laurel)	30	—35 to —20 F.	Shrub; needs acid soil
Leucothoe catesbai (fetterbush)	6	—20 to —10 F.	Shrub; good autumn color

Botanical and Common Name	Approx. Height in ft.	Minimum Night Temp.	Remarks
Libocedrus decurrens (California incense tree)	100	—10 to —5 F.	Fine evergreen tree
Lindera benzoin (spice bush)	15	—20 to —10 F.	Dense shrub with yellow flowers
Liquidambar styraciflua (sweetgum)	140	—10 to —5 F.	Good shape
Liriodendron tulipifera (tulip tree)	200	—20 to —10 F.	Robust grower
Magnolia acuminata (cucumber tree)	100	—20 to —10 F.	Fast-growing tree
M. grandiflora (Southern magnolia)	100	—5 to —10 F.	Semi-evergreen tree
M. macrophylla (large leaved cucumber tree)	50	—10 to —5 F.	Large-leaved tree
M. virginiana (sweet bay)	60	—10 to —5 F.	Dense green foliage; waxy white flowers
Mahonia aquifolium (holly mahonia)	3	—20 to —10 F.	Glossy-leaved shrub
Oxydendrum arboreum (sorrel tree)	75	—20 to —10 F.	Pyramidal tree with good fall color
Philadelphus indorus (mock orange)	10	—30 to —20 F.	Good upright shrub
Picea glauca (white spruce)	90	—50 to —35 F.	Tough evergreen tree
Pieris floribunda (andromeda)	6	—20 to —10 F.	Fine broad-leaved evergreen shrub
Pinus ponderosa (Western yellow pine)	150	—10 to —5 F.	Rapid growth
P. strobus (white pine)	150	—35 to —20 F.	Another good evergreen tree
Potentilla fruticosa (shrubby cinquefoil)	3	—50 to —35 F.	Shrub; stays in bloom a long time

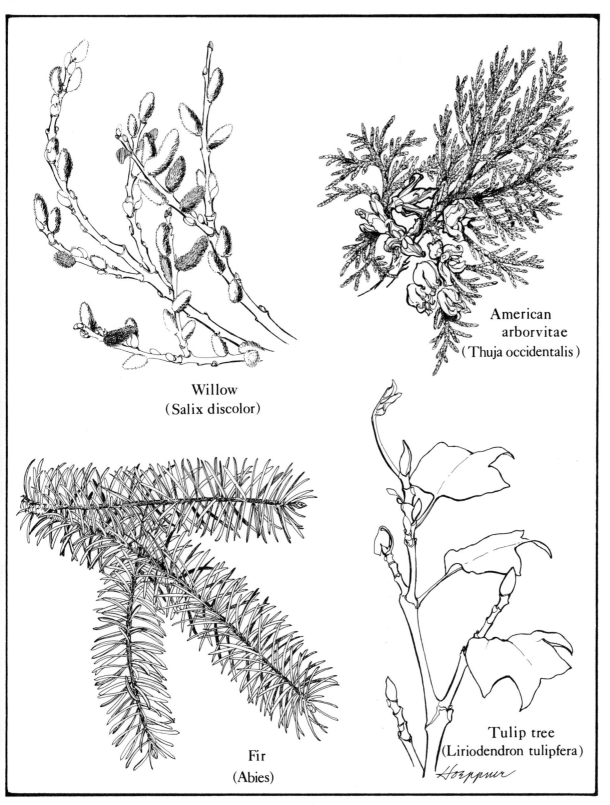

Willow
(Salix discolor)

American
arborvitae
(Thuja occidentalis)

Fir
(Abies)

Tulip tree
(Liriodendron tulipfera)

Hoeppner

Forest Trees

Botanical and Common Name	Approx. Height in ft.	Minimum Night Temp.	Remarks
Pseudotsuga menziesii (Douglas fir)	300	—10 to —5 F.	Dense pyramidal evergreen tree
Quercus alba (white oak)	100	—20 to —10 F.	Needs space
Q. coccinea (scarlet oak)	80	—20 to —10 F.	Autumn color
Robinia pseudoacacia (black acacia)	80	—35 to —20 F.	Late spring flowers
Rhododendron calendulaceum (flame azalea)	12	—10 to —5 F.	Showy native for northern gardens
R. maximum (rosebay rhododendron)	12–35	—35 to —20 F.	Tall and treelike
R. nudiflorum (pinterbloom)	6	—35 to —20 F.	Fine native of eastern United States
R. vaseyi (pinkshell azalea)	6–9	—20 to —10 F.	Does well in moist places
R. viscosum (swamp azalea)	9–12	—35 to —20 F.	Late blooming type
Rosa (many kinds)	1–5	—5 to —30 F. (depending on species)	Always popular
Salix discolor (pussy willow)	20	—35 to —20 F.	Grows in any soil
Sambucus canadensis (American elder)	12	—35 to —20 F.	Shrubs for dry or wet soil
Sorbus americana (American mountain ash)	30	—50 to —35 F.	Favorite tree
Spirea (many kinds)	5–9	—20 to —10 F.	Beautiful shrub
Symphoricarpus albus (snowberry)	5	—20 to —10 F.	Woodsy shrubs with white berries
Taxus brevifolia (Western yew)	45	—50 to —35 F.	Popular evergreen
T. canadensis (ground hemlock)	6	—50 to —35 F.	Tough plant

Botanical and Common Name	Approx. Height in ft.	Minimum Night Temp.	Remarks
Thuja occidentalis (American arborvitae)	60	—50 to —35 F.	A favorite evergreen
Tilia americana (American linden)	120	—50 to —35 F.	White flowers in summer
Tsuga canadensis (Northern hemlock)	90	—35 to —20 F.	A shrub for hedges
T. caroliniana (Southern hemlock)	75	—30 to —10 F.	Good evergreen
Vaccinum corymbosum (swamp blueberry)	15	—35 to —20 F.	Deciduous shrub
Viburnum acerfolium (maple leaf virburnum)	6	—35 to —20 F.	Shrub that can tolerate shade
V. dentatum (arrowwood viburnum)	15	—50 to —35 F.	Shrub for any soil
V. lantata (hobble bush)	15	—35 to —20 F.	Stout upright shrub
V. lentago (nanny berry)	30	—25 to —20 F.	Another dense shrub

6. Gardens for All People

Just how much time you spend at your vacation home will dictate how much gardening you want to do. For example, if you are there for weekends only, you will want gardening to be at an absolute minimum—a few leisure hours. If you vacation home is a second home, then you will want to invest more time to have a lovely garden for the property.

Often people from the East go south in the winter to maintain a vacation home. The climate is warmer, and they can have a green lovely setting. These winter gardeners should try to learn something about their new places and should try gardening because it is entirely different from summer gardening in the North.

Some people leave the city in the summer to go to the country and lake, mountain and sea for a week or two each month. Summer gardeners have more time than the weekend people, and gardening can be a profitable relaxation for soul and muscle. Summer vacationers should do some kind of gardening to please their eyes as well as enhance their property.

We have been discussing people who own their own vacation homes, but there is another type of vacationer: the tenant gardener who rents or leases for a summer, winter, or any period of time. It is not necessary for him to involve himself in the gardening picture (landlords should maintain the property), but if gardening is pleasurable, there is no reason why he cannot grow some plants on a small scale. (And sometimes by caring for the property you can reduce the rental if it is agreeable with the landlord.)

THE WEEKEND GARDENER

If you are a weekend gardener, you are probably more interested in vacation sports than gardening, but after the first flush of activity you might want to relax and tend the landscape with a minimum of effort. It is possible even in one afternoon to get some flowering shrubs in the ground for spring color or in only a few hours plant some bulbs for a cheery effect. With bulbs the work is done because the flower is already in the bulb, so it is simply a question of planting. Ground covers are other easy-maintenance plants and can add great beauty to a home for little effort. And vines, too, once planted, can do wonders for a landscape plan because they offer soft cover for walls, fences, and other areas. (See Chapter 7.)

The secret of weekend gardening is to know when to get things into the ground and to have all materials—soil, plants, shovels—

A unique water garden is used for this leisure home and once established the water plants take care of themselves, affording easy weekend gardening. *(Photo Hedrich Blessing; Architect: Harris Armstrong, FAIA).*

on hand. Then it is only a question of a few hours a day to establish, over a period of time, a beautiful setting for the vacation house.

If it is a new site, of course there will be more work—too much in fact for the weekend person—so it is best to have as much of this done by hired help if at all possible. Preparing the landscape, as described in Chapter 2, takes time and work. If it is a new vacation home, do a small area at a time, and establish a plan over the years rather than tackling it all in a few months.

Whether it is an old or new site, some pruning and grooming will have to be done. If there are large trees and shrubs, let a professional do it; it is not that expensive. If you want exercise, tackle it yourself by doing a little pruning each weekend.

Do not think that vegetable gardens are too much work. Even the weekender can have fine fresh vegetables with little effort. Once

Some flowering plants are used against the house for color; the rest of the garden is an interesting combination of stone and rock for easy no-care landscaping. This garden requires little work for the vacationer. (*Photo by Roche*).

again, *plan*. Get the plants in the ground at the right time, and then let nature do the work. However, if you are in a very dry area, a water-sprinkler system will be necessary because vegetables need plenty of water to thrive.

The weekend gardener really needs plants that can fend for themselves and so should think about growing water plants. Once planted, aquatic plants grow with little care and many of the smaller water lilies and lotus are spectacular in bloom in summer. Extensive water gardens should not be considered, but do give some thought to half barrels and kegs sunk in the ground to use as water gardens or buy the plastic commercial containers now available for water gardening.

Gardening in containers and planters is another easy way for weekenders to have greenery without too much trouble. Watered thoroughly on Sunday night or early Monday morning before you

For easy gardening consider the stone and sand garden—no flowers to care for, no lawn and yet the landscaping provides a most attractive marriage of nature and plants. (*Photo by Roche*).

Gardening does not have to be on a large scale for the weekend gardener; here some container plants are used with some bamboo in background for a lovely scene that is practically maintenance free. (*Photo courtesy Western Wood Assoc.*).

leave, plants in large tubs and pots will survive until Friday when you return to your vacation spot.

THE SUMMER GARDENER

Once you, the summer gardener, are ensconced in your vacation place, your thoughts will naturally turn to the garden. You are there to enjoy and relax, and there is no better way of enjoying yourself than by sitting on a lovely patio surrounded by greenery. Try to get an early start so you can enjoy blooming flowers while you are at the vacation site. (Perhaps you can steal a weekend in late spring to get things going.)

If you are a summer resident, do put in an annual and perennial garden (petunias, zinnias, marigolds; dianthus, aster, chrysanthemum) with summer-blooming plants you can enjoy while there. This may seem like much work, but it is not. Once the initial plantings are made, perennials return year after year to bear handsome blooms, and anuuals, which live only a year, are well worth the effort because they produce such a profusion of bloom.

The character of the summer house is apt to be informal and relaxed. There is no regimentation of life or duties, so the garden too should be fashioned in the same way. There is no necessity, whether in the hills, by the sea, or in the woods, for manicured lawns, carefully trimmed hedges, or precise bloom colors or periods. The main consideration is that flowers are in color while you are there. Shrubs and trees will take care of themselves, so the area immediately near the house will be the place where most renovating and new planting will be done. This gardening can be done in a day, a week, or a few hours a couple of days a week, which leaves plenty of time for relaxing and vacationing.

The summer home by the sea or in the woods will dictate a natural landscape with many native plants. However, there is room or should be room for a small garden between the natural backdrop (trees and shrubs already there) and the home. Make this your personal garden. Lawns are not necessary, but some link between the great outdoors and the house is what you want to create. This can be done with ground covers, flower beds, or a combination of both. Paths and walks are important and should be charming, not just straight walks to the house or through the space, but rather, curved graceful arcs to lend an intimate character throughout.

Use flowering vines to bring color to the summer place. These are spectacular plants that will bloom throughout the warm months while you are there. Get them started quickly and for the first few week watch them closely. Be sure they have plenty of water. Once established they will fend for themselves. Some pruning and trimming will be necessary but this is hardly any effort for the wealth of beauty they can bring to an area. Use vines on fences, walls—wherever you want quick color. (See Chapter 7: Vines.)

The summer gardener can very well get in tune with nature, and even if a beginner, he should try to learn the plants of the area. Whether you are there a month or all summer, it is time enough to grow some flowers and some shrubs and to create a total landscape that is handsome all summer. The trick is to preplan and visit the home in spring, if at all possible, to get plants in place and started. (For specific plants for specific areas such as by the sea, hills, or in the forest see Chapter 5.)

The Winter Gardener

If you garden during the winter in your vacation or second home, you must give more consideration to the gardening problem. As explained, you are in new territory and may not be familiar with the plant life. A completely new set of gardening do's and don'ts must be learned; experience is the only teacher. Gardening can be made easier by knowing the plants of the area and remembering that gardening during the winter in places in the West or South will be different than gardening in the East or Midwest.

It is wise to visit nurseries and see plants that grow in the area, look at neighbors' gardens, and try to learn as much about the region's plant material as possible before you proceed with extensive planting. A landscape contractor or experienced nurseryman to help you plan and select plants is also a wise move. Once plants are established and the garden is growing, you can start your own care program.

Gardening in a warm climate, where the winter gardener is most apt to have a second home, follows the usual routine of plant care and maintenance. The choice of plants will be foreign to you, so start slowly. Gather information and proceed with some help from local nurseries. Make an effort to know the climate (see Chapter 3).

This hillside home uses plants in pots and is easily tended even by the tenant gardener. The picture is intimate and charming; a total retreat in the hills. (*Photo by Roger Scharmer*).

Vines and pot plants furnish a secluded nook of a vacation spot. Here again maintenance is at a minimum. (*Photo by Roger Scharmer*).

Generally, there is no need to create a dramatic landscape plan but the essentials of good landscaping—approach to the house, entertaining area, service area—should be given careful consideration. This is your home away from home and should be a retreat that is complete with greenery and places to relax in a garden setting.

More than any other kind of vacationing gardener, the winter resident should plan a total landscape; keep it simple, sure, but at the same time make it functional and handsome.

If your vacation home is a condominium, there will be less gardening because most of the planting is done for you, other than the patio or terrace area which is usually left for the owner to landscape.

The Tenant Gardener

This is the renter who leaves the city in the summer or winter to go to a quiet place. The house may be a cabin or a studio. The tenant gardener will not want to invest too much money in someone else's property but still he or she will want some greenery to make the setting handsome as well as to get back to nature. Container gardening is the answer and can be done on a small scale. Small pots of bulbs can be started early to enjoy in the summer; a few annuals can be grown in pots to bring color to the house. Evergreens in tubs will provide a handsome green note, and all these plants may be grown on a deck or at the backyard or even in the house itself. Petunias do amazingly well at sunny windows indoors. When the summer is over there is no need to move annuals back to your permanent residence since they last only a year and if you are renting again the next year, the evergreens can be left outdoors. Other potted plants you have tended can be moved to decorate your city apartment.

For $50 or so you can have a wealth of greenery and can, when the rent time is up, ask the owner if you might do some outdoor planting next year and perhaps get a break in the rent.

7. *Time-Saving Easy Plants*

No matter where you garden or how much gardening you want to do, some plants will be more helpful than others, for example, ground covers, vines, bulbs, and flowering shrubs. These are the time-savers that, once established, need little care and grow fast. Also, most can fend for themselves if you are gone a great deal of time.

Gardening with container plants is another way to have a quick garden setting without too much work. Once in containers, the plants flourish with minimal care, a definite plus for the vacation gardener.

Following are some comments on these plants (along with lists) to help you with both your garden and vacation.

GROUND COVERS

For the weekend gardener this group of robust plants offers a wealth of greenery for little effort. Once installed, ground covers need only weekly watering to thrive. (Indeed, some such as honeysuckle may thrive too much!) Generally ground covers are used in place of lawns, but they also have many and varied uses. By using a mix-and-match layout you can create some dazzling textured gardens in any area, playing light-green foliaged covers against dark-green ones. You can also use ground covers to clothe rocks and ledges and to fill barren areas with beautiful foliage. Because ground covers come in many heights, you can create a terraced effect by using them carefully; this can suit any place on the property. Essentially, ground covers can be the workhorse of the weekend garden site.

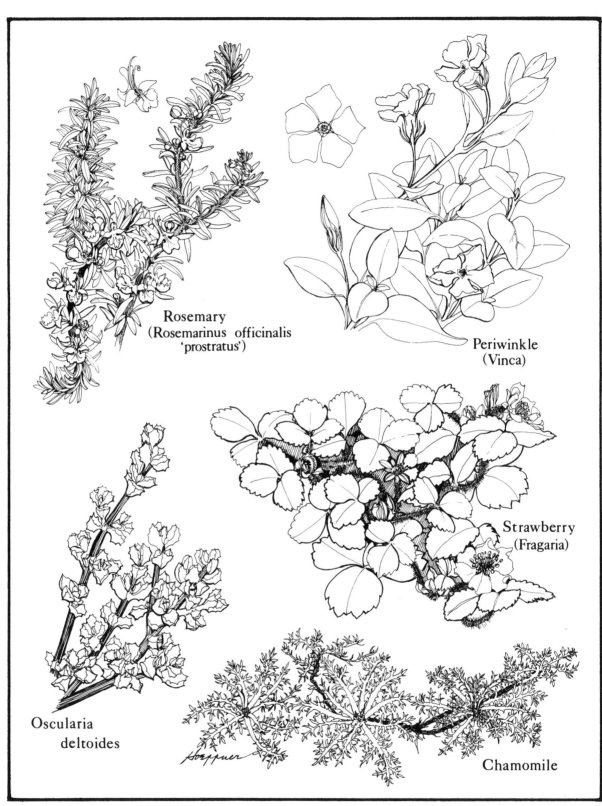

Rosemary
(Rosemarinus officinalis 'prostratus')

Periwinkle
(Vinca)

Strawberry
(Fragaria)

Oscularia
deltoides

Chamomile

Ground Covers

Planting ground covers does take some time, but if you space them closely, rather than at recommended distances, you can have a quick greenery in a few weeks instead of waiting months. For example, in California, ivy is used extensively to cover hillside areas, and the recommended planting distance is generally 12 to 18 inches. I plant ivy 4 to 6 inches apart and have a lovely green look in a few months.

Because the original planting is so important, take time with these procedures. Dig deep holes, use good top soil, and then water frequently until plants are well established. Then routine once-a-week watering is fine. Here is a list of ground covers to help you:

LIST OF GROUND COVERS

Botanical and Common Name	Height in Inches	Soil/ Moisture	Sun or Shade	Remarks
Ajuga carolinensis (bugleweed)	6	Rich soil, ample moisture	Shade	Hardy perennial; spiked blue spring flowers
Anthemis nobilis (chamomile)	3 to 5	Sandy soil, even moisture	Full sun	Lovely, with light green fernlike leaves
Arctostaphylos uva-ursi (manzanita)	12	Sandy soil, will tolerate dryness	Sun	Evergreen, with small nodding leaves
Asarum caudatum (wild ginger)	12	Rich soil, lots of moisture	Shade	Handsome, with heart-shaped leaves
Cotoneaster (many)	1 to 12	Sandy soil, will tolerate dryness	Sun	Shrubby, with small leaves and decorative berries
Dichondra carolinensis	C*	Well-drained soil, plenty of moisture	Sun	Tender; small dark-green leaves
Duchesnea indica (mock strawberry)	C	Well-drained soil, moderate moisture	Shade	Coarsely-toothed leaves; good creeper

*C denotes creepers.

Botanical and Common Name	Height in Inches	Soil/ Moisture	Sun or Shade	Remarks
Epimedium	9	Acid soil, slightly moist	Shade	Semi-evergreen with glossy leaves and dainty flowers
Erica vagans (heath)	12	Sandy soil, even moisture	Sun	Pointed needlelike leaves
Fragaria chiloensis (strawberry)	C	Well-drained soil, even moisture	Sun or shade	Small semi-evergreen leaves; white flowers; grows rapidly
Hedera helix (English ivy)	C	Any kind of soil; lots of moisture	Sun or shade	One of the most popular; some have tiny leaves and others have large foliage
Hosta (Funkia) (plantain lily)	12	Rich soil, likes water	Shade	Many varieties
Hypericum calycinum (Aaron's beard)	12	Sandy soil, will tolerate draft	Sun or shade	Prolific plant
Iberis sempervirens (candytuft)	8–12	Needs good moisture	Sun or shade	Showy in spring
Liriope muscari	12	Any type soil, good moisture	Sun or shade	Grassy foliage
Lonicera japonica ('Halliana') (honeysuckle)	6	Any type soil, will tolerate dryness	Sun or shade	Tough rampant vine, evergreen in South and semi-evergreen in North; must be kept within bounds
Mesembryan-themum (ice plant)	8	Any type of soil, will tolerate dryness	Sun	Succulent annuals or perennials; bright daisylike flowers
Oscularia deltoides	to 12	Good for dry soils	Sun	Lovely flowering ground cover

————————
*C denotes creepers.

Ground covers are at nurseries and make ideal quick cover for vacation grounds. Tiny-leaved plants such as these are ideal because they have wonderful texture and color. (*Photo by author*).

Providing a carpet of green, ground covers are excellent for the lazy gardener; once planted they fend for themselves. (*Photo by author*).

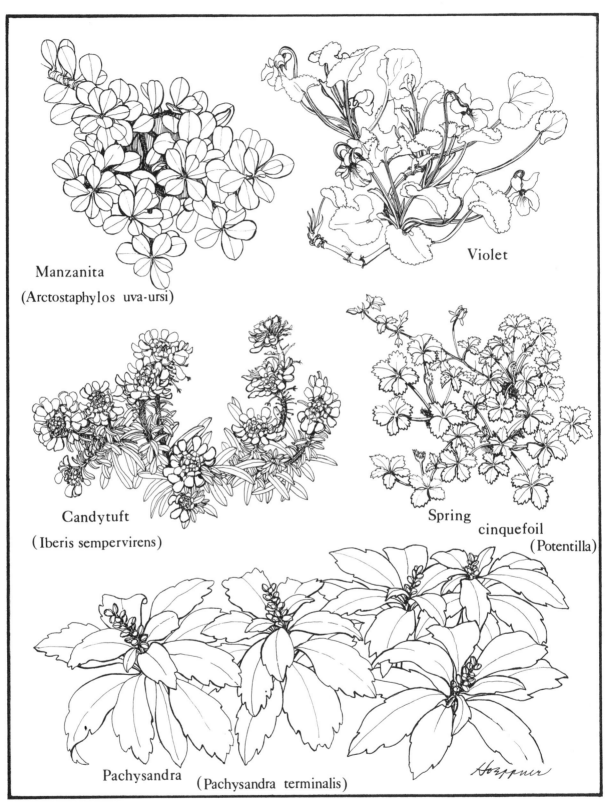

Manzanita

(Arctostaphylos uva-ursi)

Violet

Candytuft

(Iberis sempervirens)

Spring

cinquefoil

(Potentilla)

Pachysandra   (Pachysandra terminalis)

Ground Covers

Botanical and Common Name	Height in Inches	Soil/ Moisture	Sun or Shade	Remarks
Pachysandra terminalis	5 to 12	Rich soil, good moisture	Avoid sun	Slow growing; evergreen in shady areas
Potentilla (cinquefoil)	2 to 10	Rich soil	Sun, part shade	Showy cover
Rosmarinus officinalis 'Prostratus' (rosemary)	12	Tolerates poor soil, moderate moisture	Sun	Evergreen; blue spring flowers
Sedum amecamecanum (stonecrop)	C	Any type soil, moderate moisture	Sun	Low-growing, fleshy succulent
Thymus (thyme)	C	Tolerates poor soil, dry conditions	Sun	Fast grower
Viola (violet)	6–10	Rich, moist soil	Sun, partial shade	Many varieties
Vinca minor (periwinkle)	C*	Good soil, good moisture	Shade	Evergreen creeper; showy white or blue spring flowers

*C denotes creepers.

BULBS

The beauty of bulbs is hard to resist. These fine plants need only planting to produce their colorful flowers. Crocus and daffodils multiply without effort on your part, and even if subject to drought, most bulbs can pull through to produce bloom. The way to success with bulbs is to get them into the ground at the right time; with careful planting you can have spring, summer, or fall blooms in profusion.

You can use bulbs almost anywhere you want color, but do group many in one area rather than just a few, which always creates a spotty effect. Be extravagant and grow masses of bulbs. You will not be sorry because this is easy gardening and the rewards are vast. Here are some bulbs and their planting times:

A close-up showing the beauty of daffodils; these can greet you in early spring in your vacation place if you take time to plant them in late fall.

SPRING-FLOWERING BULBS

Botanical and Common Name	When to Plant	Depth in Inches	Sun or Shade	Remarks
Allium (flowering onion)	Fall	3	Sun	Prettier than you think
Chionodoxa (glory of snow)	Fall	3	Sun	Do not disturb for several years
Crocus (jonquil, narcissus)	Fall	3	Sun	Always dependable
Daffodil (jonquil, narcissus)	Fall	6	Sun	The name daffodil is used for all members

Eranthis (winter aconite)	Early fall	3	Shade	Very early bloom
Erythronium (dogtooth violet)	Early fall	6	Shade	Good for naturalizing
Fritillaria	Fall	4	Shade	Overlooked but lovely
Galanthus (snowdrop)	Fall	3	Shade	Blooms while snow is on the ground
Hyacinthus (hyacinth)	Fall	6–8	Sun	Protect from wind and ice
Iris	Fall	½ to 1	Sun	Many kinds
Leucojum (snowflake)	Fall	3	Shade	Flowers last a long time
Muscari (grape hyacinth)	Early fall	3	Sun	Easy to grow
Scilla	Fall	2	Sun or light shade	Once established blooms indefinitely
Tulipa (tulip)	Fall	6	Sun	Many kinds

You have to go a long way to beat the beauty of tulips in a natural setting. These are excellent flowers for the vacation gardener because once planted they will grow on their own. (*Photo by Molly Adams*).

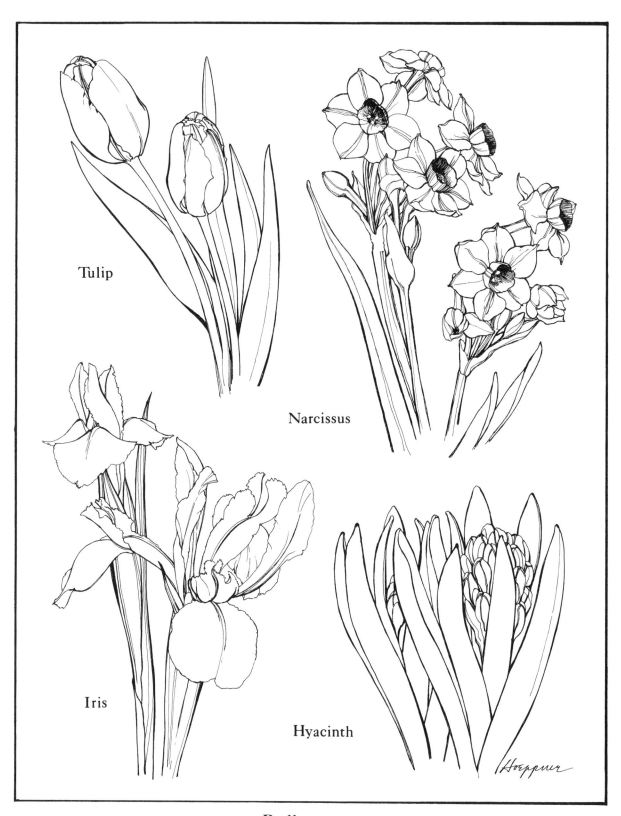

Tulip

Narcissus

Iris

Hyacinth

Bulbs

SUMMER-FLOWERING BULBS

Botanical and Common Name	Depth, In.	Sun or Shade	Remarks
Agapanthus (flower-of-the-Nile)	1	Sun	New dwarf varieties available
Alstroemeria	4	Sun	Good cut flowers
Caladium	4	Shade	Lovely foliage plants; many varieties
Canna	2	Sun	Showy flowers; lift bulbs after frost kills tops
Galtonia (summer hyacinth)	6	Sun	Buy new bulbs yearly
Polianthus tuberosa (tuberose)	1	Sun	Plant after danger of frost
Sprekelia formosissima	3	Sun	Good in pots
Ranunculus	1	Sun	Lovely colorful flowers
Tigridia (tiger flower)	2 to 3	Sun	Plant in early May
Tritonia (montbretia)	2 to 3	Sun	Plant in early May
Zephyranthes (zephyr lily)	1	Sun or light shade	Plant after danger of frost

FLOWERING SHRUBS

For privacy and color, flowering shrubs are excellent and do not require constant care. Once established, plants such as forsythia, lilac, and spiraea only need occasional pruning and feeding to grow lavishly.

Shrubs can define property lines and provide background color for other plants. They can also act as privacy hedges and are excellent for spring color to greet you at your vacation home.

LIST OF FLOWERING SHRUBS

Botanical and Common Name	SE D E	Approx. Height in ft.	Average Min. Temp.	Remarks
Abeliophyllum distichum (Korean white forsythia)	SE	5	—10 to —5 F.	Free flowering
Amelanchier canadensis (shadblow service berry)	D	30	—20 to —10 F.	Prune after bloom
Buddleia alternifolia (fountain buddleia)	D	12	—10 to —5 F.	Graceful; branching
Buddleia davidii (butterfly bush)	D/SE	15	—10 to —5 F.	Many varieties
Callistemon citrinus (bottlebrush)	E	25	20 to 30 F.	Lovely flowers
Carissa grandiflora (natal plum)	E	15	20 to 30 F.	Spiny branching one
Carpenteria californica (California mock orange)	E	8	5 to 20 F.	Showy shrub
Ceanothus americanus (New Jersey tea)	E	3	—20 to —10 F.	For poor soil
Chaenomeles speciosa (flowering quince)	D	6	—20 to —10 F.	Lovely flowers
Clethra alnifolia (summer sweet)	D	9	—25 to —20 F.	Fragrant summer
Euonymus japonica (evergreen euonymus)	E	15	10 to 20 F.	Splendid foliage
E. latifolius	D	20	—10 to —5 F.	Vigorous grower

SE = semi-evergreen   D = deciduous   E = evergreen

Peach blossoms brighten any garden in spring and are always a welcome addition
to the scene. (*USDA photo*).

Botanical and Common Name	SE D E	Approx. Height in ft.	Average Min. Temp.	Remarks
Forsythia intermedia (border forsythia)	D	2–0	—20 to —5 F.	Deep yellow flowers
F. ovata (early forsythia)	D	8	—20 to —10 F.	Earliest to bloom and hardiest
Fothergilla major (large fothergilla)	D	2	—10 to —5 F.	Good flowers and autmn flowers
Gardenia jasminoides (cape jasmine)	E	4–6	10 to 30 F.	Fragrant
Hamamelis mollis (Chinese witch hazel)	D	30	—10 to —5 F.	Very fragrant flowers
Hibiscus rosa-sinensis (Chinese hibiscus)	E	30	20 to 30 F.	Stellar flower
H. syriacus (shrub althaea)	D	15	—10 to —5 F.	Many varieties
Hydrangea arborescens 'Grandiflora' (hills-or-snow)	D	3	—20 to —10 F.	Easy culture
Jasminum nudiflorum (winter jasmine)	D	15	—10 to 5 F.	Viny shrub; not fragrant
J. officinale (common white jasmine)	SE/D	30	5 to 10 F.	Tall-growing
Kolkwitzia amabilis (beauty bush)	D	10	—20 to —10 F.	Has many uses
Lagerstroemia indica (crape myrtle)	D	20	5 to 10 F.	Popular summer bloom
Nerium oleander (oleander)	E	15	5 to 20 F.	Popular flowering shrub
Photinia serrulata (Chinese photinia)	E	36	5 to 10 F.	Bright red berries

SE = semi-evergreen   D = deciduous   E = evergreen

Botanical and Common Name	SE D E	Approx. in ft. Height	Average Min. Temp.	Remarks
Pieris floribunda (mountain andromeda)	E	5	—20 to —10 F.	Does well in dry soil
P. japonica (Japanese andromeda)	E	9	—10 to —5 F.	Splendid color
Raphiolepis umbellata (yeddo hawthorn)	E	6	5 to 10 F.	Sun or partial shade
Skimmia japonica (Japanese skimmia)	E	4	5 to 10 F.	For shade
Spiraea arguta	D	6	—20 to —10 F.	Free flowering
S. prunifolia (bridal wreath spiraea)	D	9	—20 to —10 F.	Turn orange in fall
S. thunbergii (thunberg spiraea)	D	12	—10 to —5 F.	Arching branches
Syringa henryi 'Lutece'	D	10	—50 to —35 F.	Early June bloom

Flowering plants, like the common pear, afford lovely springtime color for gardens. (*USDA photo*).

Botanical and Common Name	SE D E	Approx. Height in ft.	Average Min. Temp.	Remarks
S. villosa (late lilac)	D	9	—50 to —35 F.	Dense upright habit
S. vulgaris (common lilac)	D	20	—35 to —20 F.	Many varieties
Viburnum davidii	E	3	5 to 10 F.	Handsome leaves
V. dentatum (arrowwood)	D	15	—50 to —35 F.	Red fall color
V. lentago (nannyberry)	D	30	—50 to —35 F.	Good background or screen plant
V. prunifolium (black haw)	D	15	—30 to —20 F.	Good specimen plant
V. sieboldii	D	30	—20 to —10 F.	Stellar performer
V. trilobum (cranberry bush)	D	12	—50 to —35 F.	Effective in winter
Weigela 'Bristol Ruby'	D	7	—10 to —5 F.	Complex hybrid
W. 'Bristol Snowflake'	D	7	—10 to —5 F.	Complex hybrid
W. florida	D	9	—10 to —5 F.	Many available
W. middendorffiana	D	1	—20 to —10 F.	Dense broad shrubs

SE = semi-evergreen   D = deciduous   E = evergreen

VINES

Vines add quick color to any vacation site and are a delight in the garden. Climbing vines like bougainvillea and clematis can, with proper care, become living screens of color. Stephanotis, sweetpea, and wisteria are other fine vines, with a fragile look of loveliness that can soften harsh garden walls and house lines.

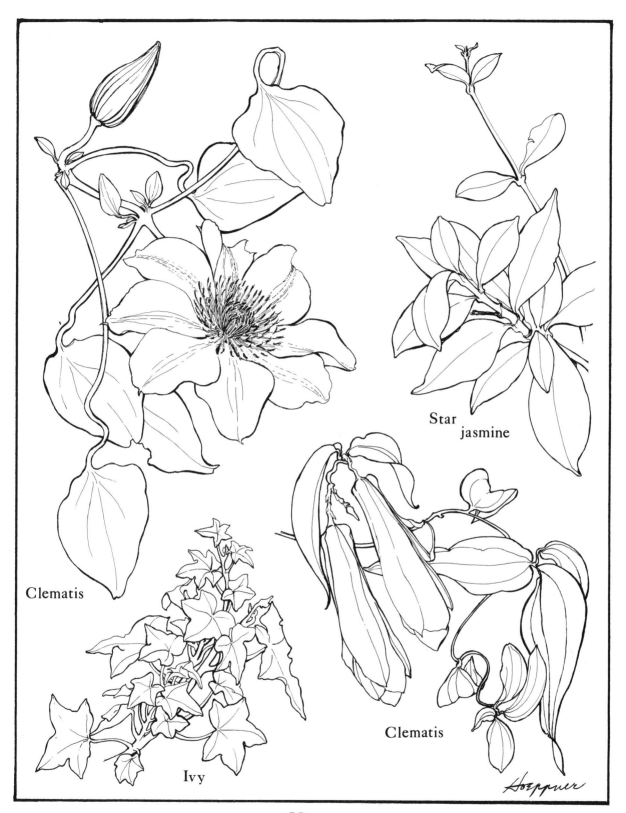

Star
jasmine

Clematis

Clematis

Ivy

Vines

Plant woody vines in deep holes to a depth of 3 to 4 feet; roots need space to grow. Use good top soil to replace dug-out soil. Water thoroughly and deeply to get plants established for the first few weeks. Then routine care is fine, say, watering once a week or more often if it does not rain.

Do not be misled into thinking that vines need constant pruning and attention—they don't. Some pruning is necessary but only at specified times of the year. The following list will guide you:

LIST OF VINES

Botanical and Common Name	Min. Night Temp.	General Description	Sun or Shade	Remarks
Akebia quinata (five-leaf akebia)	—20 to —10 F.	Vigorous twiner; fragrant small flowers	Sun or partial shade	Needs support prune in fall/ early spring
Allamanda cathartica	Tender	Dense with heavy stems, lovely tubular flowers	Sun	Prune annually in spring
Ampelopsis breviped-unculata (blueberry climber)	—20 to —10 F.	Strong grower with dense leaves	Sun or shade	Prune in early spring
Antigonon leptopus (coral vine)	Tender	Excellent as screen	Sun	Needs light support; prune hard after bloom
Aristolochia durior (Dutchman's pipe)	—20 to —10 F.	Big twiner with mammoth leaves	Sun or shade	Needs sturdy support; prune in spring or summer
Clytosoma (*Bignonia capreolata*) (cross vine) (trumpet vine)	—5 to 5 F.	Orange flowers	Sun or shade	Thin out weak branches in spring; clings by disks

Clematis is always a popular vine because it has large beautiful flowers and is dependable to bloom. Excellent for quick cover anywhere in the garden. (*Photo by author*).

Celastrus scandens (American bittersweet)	—50 to —35 F.	Light-green leaves, red berries	Sun or shade	Prune in early spring before growth starts
Clematis armandi (evergreen-clematis)	5 to 10 F.	Lovely flowers and foliage	Sun	Needs support; prune lightly after bloom
Doxantha unguis-cati	10 to 20 F.	Dark-green leaves, yellow blooms	Sun	Needs no support; prune hard after bloom
Euonymus fortunei (wintercreeper)	—35 to —20 F.	Shiny leathery leaves; orange berries in fall	Sun or shade	Needs support; prune in early spring
Fatshedera lizei	20 to 30 F.	Grown for handsome foliage	Shade	No pruning needed
Ficus pumila (*repens*) (creeping fig)	20 to 30 F.	Small heart-shaped leaves	Partial shade	Thin plant in late fall or early spring
Gelsemium sempervirens (Carolina jessamine)	Tender	Fragrant yellow flowers	Sun or partial shade	Needs support; thin plant immediately after bloom

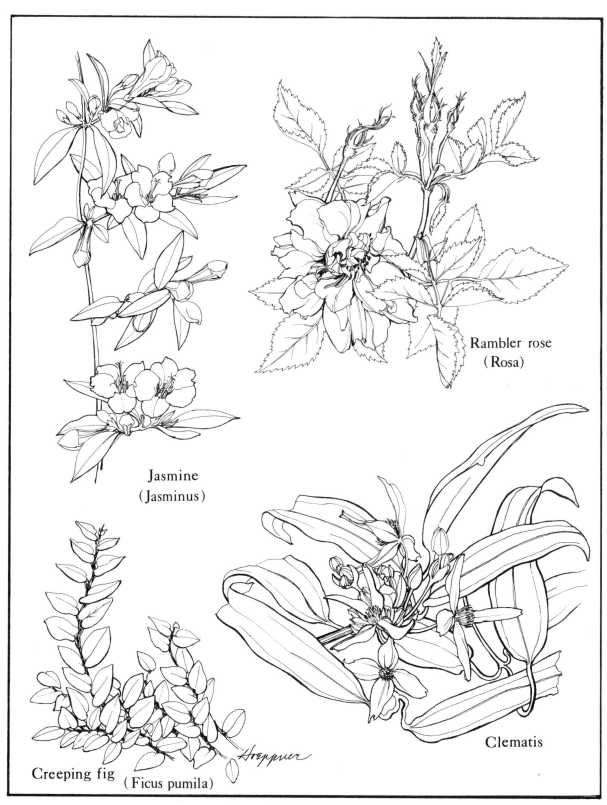

Rambler rose
(Rosa)

Jasmine
(Jasminus)

Clematis

Creeping fig (Ficus pumila)

Vines

Botanical and Common Name	Min. Night Temp.	General Description	Sun or Shade	Remarks
Hedera helix (English ivy)	−10 to −5 F.	Scalloped neat leaves; many varieties	Shade	Prune and thin in early spring
Hydrangea petiolaris (climbing hydrangea)	−20 to −10 F.	Heads of snowy flowers	Sun or partial shade	Thin and prune in winter or early spring
Ipomoea purpurea (Convolvulus) (morning glory)	Tender	Flowers are blue, white, purple, pink, or red	Sun	Bloom until frost
Jasminum nudiflorum	−10 to −5 F.	Yellow flowers	Sun or shade	Needs strong support; thin and shape annually after bloom
J. officinale (white jasmine)	5 to 10 F.	Showy dark-green leaves and white flowers	Sun or shade	Provide strong support, thin and shape after bloom
Kadsura japonica (scarlet kadsura)	5 to 10 F.	Bright red berries in fall	Sun	Needs support; prune annually in early spring
Lonicera caprifolium (sweet honeysuckle)	−10 to −5 F.	White or yellow trumpet flowers	Sun	Prune in fall or spring
L. hildebrandiana (Burmese honeysuckle)	20 to 30 F.	Shiny dark-green leaves	Sun or partial shade	Needs support; prune in late fall
L. japonica 'Halliana' (Hall's honeysuckle)	−20 to −10 F.	Deep-green leaves, bronze in fall	Sun or shade	Provide support; prune annually in fall and spring
Mandevilla suaveolens (Chilean jasmine)	20 to 30 F.	Heart-shaped leaves and flowers	Sun	Trim and cut back lightly in fall
Parthenocissus quinquefolia (Virginia creeper)	−35 to −20 F.	Scarlet leaves	Sun or shade	Prune in early spring

Botanical and Common Name	Min. Night Temp.	General Description	Sun or Shade	Remarks
Passiflora caerulea (passion flower)	5 to 10 F.	Spectacular flowers	Sun	Needs support; prune hard
Phaseolus coccineus (scarlet runner bean)	Tender	Bright red flowers	Sun	Renew each spring
Plumbago capensis (plumbago)	20 to 30 F.	Blue flowers	Sun	Prune somewhat in spring
Pueraria thunbergiana (Kudzo vine)	—5 to 5 F.	Purple flowers	Sun or partial shade	Provide sturdy support; cut back hard annually in fall
Rosa (rambler rose)	—10 to —5 F.	Many varieties	Sun	Need support; prune out dead wood, shorten long shoots, and cut laterals

Carolina jessamine makes a handsome vine with yellow flowers and is excellent for covering fences, walls. Ivy, too, is a fine vine and once established grows quickly. (*Photo by author*).

				back to two nodes in spring or early summer after bloom
Smilax rotundifolia (horse brier)	—20 to —10 F.	Good green foliage	Sun or shade	Prune hard annually any time; needs no support
Trachelospermum jasminoides (star jasmine)	20 to 30 F.	Dark-green leaves and small white flowers	Partial shade	Provide heavy support; prune very lightly in fall
Vitis coignetiae (glory grape)	—10 to 5 F.	Colorful autumn leaves	Sun or partial shade	Needs sturdy support; prune very lightly in fall
Wisteria floribunda (Japanese wisteria)	—20 to —10 F.	Violet-blue flowers	Sun	Provide support and prune annually once mature to shorten long branches after bloom or in winter; pinch back branches first year

CONTAINER GARDENING

Gardening in pots and tubs is a boon to the avid gardener. Plants in containers give quick color where and when you need it. If you have a patio, terrace, or deck, container gardening is certainly the answer to easy gardening because it allows you time to both garden and vacation. Furthermore, if soil in your area is poor, container gardening is an intelligent way to have plants you want. Almost any kind of plant can be grown in a tub or box, but some do better than others.

For the most part, container plants need copious waterings and some feeding during spring and summer. In fall and winter allow plants to rest somewhat but still keep them moist.

Here are some excellent container plants (trees and shrubs), to get you started:

TREES FOR CONTAINER GARDENING

Botanical and Common Name	Min. Night Temp.	General Description	Remarks
Acer palmatum (Japanese maple)	−10 to 0 F.	Lovely lacy leaves	Handsome in soy tub or in round container
Araucaria excelsa (Norfolk pine)	Tender	Pyramid leaves	Good vertical accent in Spanish flare-lip pot

Betula populifolia (gray birch)	—20 to —10 F.	Deciduous; ir- regular in shape	Fine patio tree or along house wall
Cedrus atlantica glauca (Blue Atlas cedar)	0 to 10 F.	Needle ever- green with sprawling habit	Fine accent in large tubs near house corners
Citrus (orange, lemon lime)	Tender	Dark-green leaves; nice branching effect	Excellent trees, indoors or out

Three tubs of evergreens accent this handsome vacation patio; the statuesque tree is also a definite asset in this easy-to-care-for retreat. (*Photo courtesy California Redwood Assoc.*).

Botanical and Common Name	Min. Night Temp.	General Description	Remarks
Eriobotrya japonica (loquat)	20 to 35 F.	Round-headed, with dark-green leaves	Good for tubs and boxes
Ficus benjamina (weeping fig)	Tender	Tiny dark-green leaves; branching habit	Good special effect in garden
Gingko biloba (gingko)	—20 to —20 F.	Deciduous; lovely foliage	Handsome in containers; nice accent near house walls
Laburnum waterei (golden chain tree)	—10 to —5 F.	Deciduous, with columnar shape	Good patio tub plant
Lagerstroemeria indica (crape myrtle)	—20 to —10 F.	Deciduous, with pink flowers	Showy for patio
Magnolia soulangiana (saucer magnolia)	—20 to —10 F.	Deciduous, with round form, lovely flowers	Good near fence or wall
Malus sargenti (Sargent crab apple)	—30 to —20 F.	Dwarf; round-topped form	Perimeter decoration for paved area
Phellodendron amurense (cork tree)	—40 to —30 F.	Deciduous, attractive branching tree	For a special place
Phoenix roebellini (date palm)	Tender	Lovely arching fronds	An indoor-outdoor plant
Pinus mugo mughas (mugho pine)	—40 to —30 F.	Irregular outline, broad and sprawling	To decorate paths, walks, and patios
Pinus parviflora glauca (Japanese white pine)	—10 to —5 F.	Needle evergreen, with horizontal growth	Nice feature in and around garden
Pinus thunbergii (Japanese black pine)	—20 to —10 F.	Good spreading habit	Excellent container plant

Podocarpus gracilior	Tender	Graceful willowy branches	Good doorway plant
Rhapis excelsa (lady palm)	Tender	Dark-green fan-shaped leaves	A stellar container plant
Salix matsudana tortuosa (contorted Hankow willow)	−20 to −10 F.	Lovely sweeping branches	For a special place
Schefflera acontifolia (Australian umbrella tree)	Tender	Graceful stems tipped with fronds of leaves	Handsome in terra-cotta Spanish pot

Container gardens add much beauty to a vacation rental and can be moved about at will. There is no necessity to dig or spade, only to water the plants a few times a week. (*Photo by Matthew Barr*).

SHRUBS FOR CONTAINER GARDENING

Botanical and Common Name	Min. Night Temp.	General Description	Remarks
Abutilon (flowering maple)	Tender	Bell-shaped flowers of paper-thin texture	Give plenty of water and sun
Azalea (See Rhododendron)	Check with nursery	Brilliant flowers; lush growth	Great for portable gardens
Camellia japonica (common camellia)	5 to 10 F.	Handsome flowers in many colors	Another excellent container plant
C. sasanqua (sasanqua camellia)	5 to 10 F.	Mostly small white flowers	Many varieties
Cotoneaster (many varieties)	Check with nursery	Glossy leaves; colorful berries	Small and large ones
Fatsia japonica (aralia)	Tender	Foliage plant, with fan-like leaves on tall stems	Makes bold appearance
Gardenia jaminoides (cape jasmine)	10 to 30 F.	Dark-green leaves and fragrant white blooms	New blooming varieties available
Hibiscus rosa-sinensis (Chinese hibiscus)	20 to 30 F.	Glossy dark-green foliage; large flowers	Good performer in tubs or boxes
Juniperus chinensis 'Pfitzeriana' (Pfitzer juniper)	−20 to −10 F.	Blue-green foliage	Good screen plant
J. communis depressa (prostrate juniper)	−50 to −35 F.	Blue-green foliage	Forms dense mass
Ilex crenata (holly)	−5 to 5 F.	Glossy leaves; bright berries	Many good varieties
Ixora (star flower)	Tender	Small red flowers	Splendid color in white tubs

Nerium oleander (oleander)	10 to 20 F.	Dark-green leaves and bright flowers	Needs large container and lots of water
Osmanthus ilcifolius (holly olive)	—5 to 5 F.	Glossy leaves on upright stems	Grows fast in tubs
Pittosporum tobira	10 to 20 F.	Arching branches	Can be trained to shape
Plumbago capensis (blue phlox)	20 to 30 F.	Small leaves and blue flowers	Robust grower
Podocarpus macrophyllus	Tender	Bright green leaves	Attractive in tubs
Rhododendron (many varieties)	Check with nursery	Many varieties	Excellent container plants
Rosa (many varieties)	Check with nursery	All kinds and colors	Do very well in containers
Thuja occidentalis (arborvitae)	—50 to —35 F.	Evergreens	Tough plants for untoward conditions
Viburnum (many varieties)	Check with nursery	Attractive leaves; pretty flowers and berries	Many varieties
Yucca filamentosa (Spanish bayonet) (Adam's needle)	—20 to —10 F.	Blue-green sword-shaped leaves	Dramatic in tubs

8. Condominium and Mobile Home Landscaping

A condominium is a multitype dwelling in which homeowners own their own units and the land directly underneath—townhouses, some apartments—and then with other owners have joint ownership of all property, for example, walkways and parking areas. The landscaping around the complex is predetermined, but many condominium townhouses have a backyard or patio area or an atrium, and the apartment units usually have balconies for gardening. Generally the patio or court is walled for privacy and may be large or small. In any case, these areas afford the homeowner a place to garden at leisure.

Although the patio or allotted garden area is already walled or fenced, the homeowner must supply all soil and plant materials and do his own garden or outdoor room. But the patio garden gives you greenery and offers low maintenance and care, and it can be landscaped in several different ways, depending upon the personal taste of the owner and the dictates of money.

Balconies for gardening are usually small, but recently builders have enlarged these areas; here is a perfect place to do container gardening. Growing plants in tubs and boxes is an easy way to have a few plants do a lot for you, and, again, care is at minimum.

The Patio Garden

A patio or terrace in the home needs planning and design because even if it is used for only a few months in the year, it serves as another room. Before deciding what and where to plant, decide what it will be. The size and your personal needs will dictate what

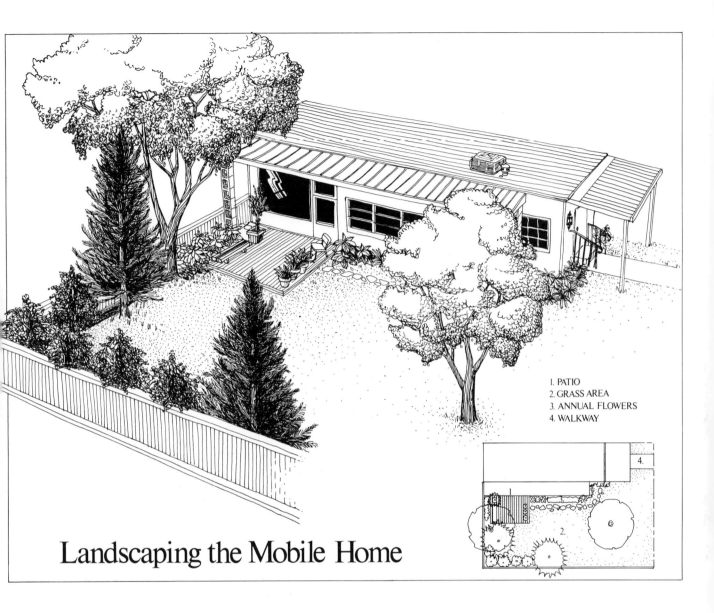

1. PATIO
2. GRASS AREA
3. ANNUAL FLOWERS
4. WALKWAY

Landscaping the Mobile Home

kind of outdoor living area to have. It can be a simple exposed patio, with plants adjacent to the home to provide a handsome picture to make the room look larger. If you enjoy outdoor cookery and dining, it can be a fully enclosed or partially roofed terrace convenient to the dining room or the kitchen. A terrace can also be a walled area off the bedroom, decorated with flowering plants.

Pavings. The first consideration for the patio is the floor; walls (if not already in place) and ceilings (canopies, arbors, overhangs) can be built later. Look at all types of pavings at material supply yards and garden centers before making a decision. Industry offers a wide selection for outdoor flooring materials. Choose carefully; select a paving that is in character with your home. A patio floor may be concrete, but it can also be brick or flagstone for a dramatic picture, or tile for long-lasting beauty.

Before making your final decision about the patio floor, ask yourself these questions:

1. Will the paving withstand weather and wear?
2. Will it be easy to maintain?
3. Is the floor comfortable to walk on? Is it so rough that it might injure children's knees?
4. Does water sink through the paving, or does it flow off in sheets, making it slippery?
5. Should the paving be light in color or dark? Light paving creates a glare; dark paving stores up heat. And, finally, think about the cost and the installation fee.

Concrete may not be as handsome as some other pavings, but it is a durable, low-cost, and very permanent surface. It is easy to clean, and if you object to its cold feeling, mix it with color or cover it with paint or dye the top layer with liquid, which will seep deeply into the pores of the concrete. The concrete can also be rough or textured.

An aggregate floor is another idea. It is made of concrete that has small stones on the surface. The textured finish is handsome and blends with plantings and lawns. The uneven texture breaks the monotony of a large area of paving, especially when it is framed with wood grids. The pebbly surface of aggregate concrete also eliminates glare and guarantees sure traction in wet weather. And when this paving collects dirt—as it will—it is easy to clean with a strong hosing.

The slick, or hard finish is made by moving a steel trowel over the surface when it is partially hardened. Do the first troweling lightly, just enough to smooth the float texture. Then trowel again with more pressure. This floor is slick and somewhat uninteresting.

The wood-float method leaves a floor smooth but not shiny. It is done with the mason's wood trowel (float).

A patio garden of a condominium combines a seating area with a garden for vacation pleasure. Note vines started on walls. (*Photo by Gary Brant.*)

An olive tree and tree-top sculpture make this attractive vacation garden most appealing. Maintenance is minimal and yet there is enough color to provide a pleasant view. (*Photo by Gary Brant*).

Most condominiums have their atrium or patio areas where the owner can establish his own personal garden. (*Photo courtesy American Plywood Assoc.*).

The broom finish gives an interesting texture. It is made by brushing the slightly hardened concrete with a push broom.

Brick is the most popular paving material, probably it is difficult to commit a serious error when paving with it. By using the simple method of brick on sand it is easy to take up the section and relay it if the first attempt is not pleasing or accurate.

Brick comes in a variety of earthy colors that look good outdoors and impart a pleasant contrast in texture. There are rough and smooth-surfaced brick, glazed or unglazed. Other shapes are available too: hexagon, octagon, fleur-de-lis. Because the units are small, they never steal the show, and they stay in scale with even the smallest foliage display.

There are many kinds of brick, but the best ones for patios are smooth-surfaced or rough-textured common brick. Face brick, including Roman and paving brick, is easier to work with and less expensive then slick brick. Common brick is usually available with pit marks on the surace. Sand-mold brick is smooth-textured and slightly larger on one face than on the other, and clinker brick has irregularities on the surface. If you can, select hard-burned rather than green brick. It should be dark red in color rather than salmon, which indicates an underburned process and less durability. Used bricks or colored ones are fine too. When you select the brick flooring be sure the dealer has a sufficient quantity to complete the area because there is usually some dimensional variation and color difference in later orders of brick. If you are in a climate where winters are severe, specify SW (severe weathering) brick.

Bricks can be laid in a great variety of patterns—herringbone, basket weave, running bond, and so on—or combined with squares of grass or cinders in endless designs. For large areas, choose the herringbone pattern; smaller patios look best with running bond or basket weave designs. Or break the large area by fitting bricks into redwood or cedar grid patterns. Bricks can also be set in mortar, but this is usually a job for the professional bricklayer.

Planning and Planting.   You will find that a small condominium patio garden not only delights the eye but also means minimal gardening to keep you active and to create your own private Eden.

In condominium living the tendency of many buildings in a cluster often coaxes the owner to provide greenery for the eye and satisfaction for the soul. And walled patio gardening is a delight to do. As your own special place, it is worth its space in gold.

As mentioned, a hard surface floor most likely will already have been installed by the contractor. If possible, and you get there first, have him leave planting pockets for plants. This breaks the monotony of a solid paved area, and plants look good used in this way because they seem to belong rather than just being placed. Use two large planting pockets (for tree, perhaps) as accents, and place smaller planter beds along one wall for perennials and annuals. You do want plants in the patio, of course, but you do not want a jungle

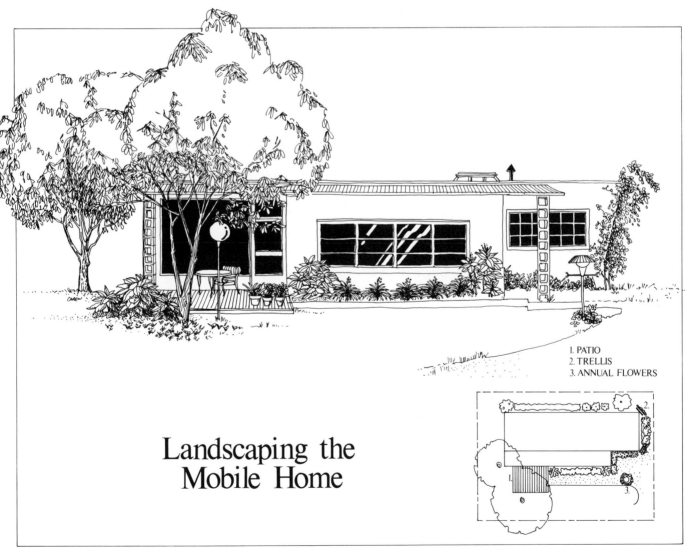

1. PATIO
2. TRELLIS
3. ANNUAL FLOWERS

Landscaping the Mobile Home

here because you will often use the patio as an extra room for entertaining. So a few specimen types, a minimum of shrubbery, and a flower bed is really all that is required.

Plan the private garden with consideration of line and detail. In the outdoors, where there is a natural background, you can get away with a few mistakes, but not here. You will be working in a confined area, so you need to have every plant perfect and superbly chosen. Do search for that perfect olive tree with gnarled branches and sweeping graceful lines as an accent, and do select full bushy shrubs that will add low horizontal thrust to the scene. And provide seasonal color with perennials and annuals in suitable planters or in the ground of spaces that have been left open in the paved area. Later you can add some stunning pot plant specimens to be used outdoors in good weather and indoors in cold weather to provide decoration.

A place to sit, some benches, and perhaps some statuary can transform the condominium garden into a visual treat you can be proud of, and taking care of the plants will entail only a few hours a week. Because the patio floor of your condominium is already paved, you are forced to use container plants unless you want to dig up some paving. Plants in containers— and almost any plant can be grown in a pot for some time—will allow you to decorate the area in little time. Select ornamental tubs and boxes (there are dozens now at suppliers) and choose small, graceful trees. Grow bulbs and perennials and some annuals in planter boxes (which can be made from redwood), for that important seasonal color. Shrubs in containers will look their best trimmed and pruned frequently, so be aware of this when planning the container garden. Once again, house plants and trees of all kinds can be used in the patio in handsome tubs when weather permits and returned indoors for winter decoration.

Use line and balance within your patio, selecting vertical plants as well as low massing horizontal ones to balance the scene. For the best results, group planters and tubs together—say three tubs to an area—so you can provide a good display rather than a lone tub that will give a spotty effect. Groups of six or ten small pots with plants are handsome, and do make them all the same kind rather than ten plants in one large tub. Search out the really orna-

This mobile home landscape uses gravel chips for easy maintenance; plants are sparse but well-chosen. (*Photo by Matthew Barr*).

mental urns and jardinieres rather than the usual wooden ones. A certain amount of decorative flair is needed to make the patio garden a stellar one.

Caring for your plants in the patio garden is merely a question of sufficient watering and moderate feeding. Plants in tubs and boxes will need more water than those directly in the ground, and, in all cases, a sensible feeding and grooming program will keep everything in top shape.

BALCONY GARDENS

Narrow balconies give the gardener little space for living plants. Yet these long areas can be cleverly camouflaged to appear like green havens. It is not easy but it can be done. Vines and trailers are essential to cover bare walls, to decorate railings, and, in some cases, to provide privacy from close-by neighbors. A small canvas or fiberglass awning is sometimes desirable, but you should first check with the building superintendent to see if this structure is allowed.

Pots of seasonal flowering plants are indispensable for balcony gardens. Do not use one large pot; group several small ones together for a colorful display. If there is space, you might want window boxes on the sides of the balcony. A hanging basket on the wall, perhaps two, is another note of decoration. Often there is not enough space for much more on the narrow balcony. Yet even this small greenery is a welcome sight on a crowded street of brick buildings.

MOBILE HOMES

Mobile homes are apt to be confused with a trailer or camper. Actually, they are small factory-built house delivered to a site. That they do have wheels to get them to the site has confused the issue somewhat. Once on the property, the mobile home is placed on a pier foundation and connected to water and electrical systems; there the home stays until the owner decides to leave, in which case wheels are attached and the home is moved somewhere else. Portability is its asset, and these mobile homes can be as large as 1,500 square feet, the size of an average house.

This fine example of landscaping makes a mobile home a lovely scene. Lawn and ground cover and bamboo along the home create a handsome setting. (*Photo by Matthew Barr*).

As vacation retreats, mobile homes serve a definite purpose: Each year you can choose your own location and enjoy a multitude of climates. The major problem with mobile homes is that they are not welcome everywhere because even though they may be lovely outside and inside, once set on a piece of land they appear out of place. On land, more than anywhere else, some kind of temporary or permanent landscaping is necessary to make the mobile home visually acceptable. At first this may seem a chore, but one of my assistants who has a mobile home proved to me it is possible to transform these homes on wheels into a lovely picture. In a few months time she added a small grass area, pebbled paths, and some container plants. Approaching her home one does feel it is a home and not just a structure placed on a hunk of land.

A small lawn area around the sides and front of a mobile home softens the somewhat severe appearance. Such a small expanse of lawn does not cost much and can be accomplished in a relatively short time. Stones and pebbles (other inexpensive materials) can also work wonders in providing a softening effect for the home. And rather than put plants into the ground, they can be in containers so they can be moved at will. Such a landscaping is hardly complete, but it offers enough greenery to make the total scene attractive.

For privacy, hedges on each side of the mobile home may be a sound idea even though these must be in the ground. The cost, about $40, will be well worth the expenditure. Small window boxes and planters are other added touches that can bring greenery to the mobile home situation.

Planting and Planning.   The best approach to the planning of the mobile home garden is to frame the house on three sides; make it an entity in itself. Plants can do the job for you better than anything else. Plants also provide privacy in such situations. Do not be afraid to use some tall hedge shrubs and an occasional small tree to give dimension to the site.

Container gardening again comes to the rescue, and you can grow almost any plant you want in this manner. Keep the plan simple but attractive. Too many plants will require too much care and make the site seem forced rather than natural. But a few well-chosen

Container plants make an attractive entry for this mobile home. All kinds of plants can be grown in tubs and pots and do very well. (*Photo by Matthew Barr*).

plants in specific areas—especially corners near the mobile—can add great beauty.

Pebble walks and stone areas are other ways of providing attractiveness for the mobile home without adding work to your daily schedule. Do not try to have everything on the mobile home site; use well-chosen plants that you like.

Any vacation place, as we have shown throughout this book, can become beautiful with carefully selected plants that provide greenery and color and make the vacation or second home a place you will want to come to. Barren sites are hardly handsome, so pitch in with soil and plants and you will be amazed at what you can accomplish in a short time without much cost or labor.